THE DARKEST PARTS OF MY BLACKNESS

Maurice Tyree

and

Katie Singer

THE DARKEST PARTS OF MY BLACKNESS

A Journey of Remorse, Reform, Reconciliation, and (R)evolution

The Carceral Studies Collection

Collection Editors
Ian Cummins & Louis Mendoza

First published in 2024 by Lived Places Publishing

All rights reserved. No part of this publication may be reproduced, stored in a retrieval system, or transmitted in any form or by any means - electronic, mechanical, photocopy, recording or otherwise - without prior permission in writing from the publisher.

The authors and editors have made every effort to ensure the accuracy of information contained in this publication, but assumes no responsibility for any errors, inaccuracies, inconsistencies and omissions. Likewise, every effort has been made to contact copyright holders. If any copyright material has been reproduced unwittingly and without permission, the Publisher will gladly receive information enabling them to rectify any error or omission in subsequent editions.

Copyright © 2024 Maurice Tyree and Katie Singer

British Library Cataloguing in Publication Data
A CIP record for this book is available from the British Library

ISBN: 9781915734297 (pbk)
ISBN: 9781915734310 (ePDF)
ISBN: 9781915734303 (ePUB)

The rights of Maurice Tyree and Katie Singer to be identified as the Authors of this work have been asserted by them in accordance with the Copyright, Design and Patents Act 1988.

Cover design by Fiachra McCarthy
Book design by Rachel Trolove of Twin Trail Design
Typeset by Newgen Publishing UK

Lived Places Publishing
Long Island
New York 11789

www.livedplacespublishing.com

Abstract

Maurice Tyree went to prison thinking that life was disposable. He came out knowing that he had a story to tell.

This is his story, told through letters and poems written during and since his time in prison. An honest and reflective narrative, this epistolary autoethnography provides a glimpse into the experience of a person who committed and served time for premeditated murder, and used his time incarcerated to reflect on and transform his life.

Ideal reading for students of Incarceration or Carceral Studies, Criminal Justice, Social Work and Family Studies, Sociology, Literature, and related courses, Mr Tyree offers first-hand insight to the experience of the US criminal legal system as an African American man.

Key words

Incarceration; carceral studies; African American; jail; criminal justice; autobiography; epistolary; poetry; transformation; literature

In honor of my fallen comrades, for whom's cause I haven't been perfect within, though, have been faithful unto;

Shirley E. Tyree (Grandma)
Maybell T. Henderson-Chase (Ma)
Charles F. Tyree (Dad)
Tawana R. Harden (Sis)

To you I dedicate this collection of letters..

To the destruction of your enemies, poverty, drugs, and disease, I dedicate my life.

This book is dedicated to the victim(s) of my crime.

From the Quran:

"I would desire that you be laden with my sin and with your sin,[50] and thus become among the inmates of the Fire. That indeed is the right recompense of the wrong-doers.

At last his evil soul drove him to the murder of his brother, and he killed him, whereby he himself became one of the losers.

Thereupon Allah sent forth a raven who began to scratch the earth to show him how he might cover the corpse of his brother. So seeing he cried: 'Woe unto me! Was I unable even to be like this raven and find a way to cover the corpse of my brother?[51] Then he became full of remorse at his doing.[52]

Therefore We ordained for the Children of Israel[53] that he who slays a soul unless it be (in punishment) for murder or for spreading mischief on earth shall be as if he had slain all mankind; and he who saves a life shall be as if he had given life to all mankind.[54] And indeed again and again did Our Messengers come to them with clear directives; yet many of them continued to commit excesses on earth."

-Surah 5:29-32

Author's Note

At the request of my publisher, I shall state that these writings are my own views, for which some have changed significantly. Transformation, processing in mind, in body, and in spirit subsequently reforms perspectives.

Nonetheless, to my endeared readers, I have attempted to offer you a rare opportunity to view another individuals' quest for social liberation.

Publisher's Note

The content presented herein is based on the author's perspective and experiences. The views and perspectives of the author are not necessarily those of the publisher. Our role as a publisher is to ensure many and varied voices are heard openly and unfiltered and that diverse life experiences find expression in our books. We support our authors fiercely, but we do not always share their opinions or perspectives.

Contents

Content warning	xii
Learning objectives	xiii
Introduction: letter to the court	1
Chapter 1 Fending for myself	27
Chapter 2 No more keeping it to myself	59
Chapter 3 Sankofa	105
Chapter 4 Cousins, comrades, cellies, friends, and teachers	159
Chapter 5 Letter of resignation	249
Chapter 6 "Mental health's undocumented and oppressive continuum"	261
Recommended projects	324
Notes	326
References	331
Recommended further reading	337
Index	339

Content warning

This book contains explicit references to, and descriptions of, situations which may cause distress. This includes references to and descriptions of:

- Suicidal thoughts, intentions, and actions
- Drug abuse
- Physical violence

This is the story of prison life; consequently, references to potentially distressing topics will occur frequently throughout the book.

Learning objectives

1. Readers will gain a nuanced understanding of the American prison system.
2. Readers will gain insight into the role of resiliency in life experience.
3. Readers will understand that varying life perspectives are based on life experiences.
4. Readers will understand the impact of early education experiences on a person's life.
5. Readers will come away with a humanized perspective on prison life.

Introduction: letter to the court

FORWARD

Your Honorable Judge Robert I. Richter:

My name is Maurice W. Tyree (Case No. F4311-01), and I was tried and sentenced by this Court for, first degree premeditated murder and related offences. I was 27 years of age then, and I am now 47 years of age.

Amid these many years, I have, with a heavy heart, wanted to write and address this Court with my gratitude for its' impartiality during the entire afore-mentioned proceedings. And, to express my mental and physical progress.

First and foremost, I must acknowledge an atonement. That the act of murder of another human being is unjustifiable. I was wrong. The victimization of this man and the psychological effect it had on his family was senseless and inexcusable.

Although I accepted responsibility in my heart a long time ago, I have learned that remorse itself is different. It took time for the toxins in the humanistic values and concerns of a hazardous individual to be removed. Thereafter, it required the cooperation of both upright thoughts and actions. In essence it is a transformation…a process.

Furthermore, for reasons that may be strange to only me, it was not until June 25, 2003, during my sentencing hearing, that I began to question, in full view, my thought process and behaviors. Your Honor allowed me to speak so that I could address the Court. I did. Thereafter, you addressed me directly. I cannot remember much of what was said in general that morning, though, I remember how a few words that you spoke made me feel, as well as, reflect thenceforth.

> Here I quote, in rendition, that which you stated;

> "Mr. Tyree, I believe that you have a good side to you… however, you also have this bad side as well…"

It yet and still amazes me how much someone that does so much wrong can never realize it. We believe even with all the chaos inflicted by us, that we are rightfully justified. Your statement was not only the beginning of my prison term, but the beginning of my induction into accepting responsibility and considering the lifetime experiences of remorsefulness after repentance.

Mental/Education

This conviction was my first major offense as an adult, as well as, my first time doing a lengthy prison term. Prior, I had been committed for 30 days as a juvenile, rendering me completely unprepared for what would be to follow. Obviously, I was afraid, which could be considered normal, yet I was also uneducated. In the world of academia, I would have been classified as; functional illiterate. As such, I could hardly comprehend the reality I was accustomed to, let alone, the paralysis of this new reality. I learned immediately that this new reality had zero offering of a chance to be formally educated. Later I even found out that the penitentiary also was pseudo-equipped to compliment the educational needs of myself. This heightened the anger in which I possessed already.

I am embarrassed to inform you that anger have always punished me. Anger is very difficult to restrain, and is a laborious burden on the heart and mind. Mine was compounded with a stern output of aggression, which I've equated to my then inability to articulate my feelings and words properly. Organizing my anger, and obtaining my education was a matter of self and social preservation. I realized that I had to save myself, and, possibly others.

I searched and searched. I searched myself and every possible external sign post that resembled a finish line to the marathon that my soul had been running. That finish line that would relieve me from all the layers of circumstantial and factual burdens. Burden, founded by my mother's drug addicted body, which warranted my premature birth. Burden, agitated by her physical abuse on my toddler frame that sent me occasionally to the emergency room to repair my tiny bones. Burden, by having to live with my paternal grandmother, in order to save my life. Burden by, being odd, angry, small, violent, abused, an abuser, orphaned, unloved, uneducated, unskilled, a child-father, a convicted murderer, a junkie, and most immeasurably, burdened, by suffering from all the inarticulate bundle of confusion that plagued my life.

During my own addiction to heroin, which I fell into while incarcerated, I encroached upon a line that administered some authentic relief. I fell yet again into another habit. I taught myself how to read, comprehend, and to write. First, with auto-biographies, which helped me to unravel the contents of my very own life. The similarity and feats in the lives of others amazed my curiosity. Next, philosophy, aphorisms, and poetry, for which I have not yet encountered one of the other that I find disliking.

The habitual adventure did not end there. Subsequently, I desired to explore writing. I wrote about what I had read. I wrote about my environment. I wrote intimately about my family. Then, I started writing more and more about my thoughts of myself. Each day I flung from my soul those unapologetic and forbidden words against myself. Words filled with accusations and self-hatred. A storm of words that crushed through the padlocked veil that supported and separated me from my very own self-awareness and the rest of society. Your Honor, as I wrote life continued to open up to me. Literature literally transformed me into a better man.

To date, I do not possess a formal education(high school diploma, G.E.D., etc.). The Bureau of Prisons' Education

Department focuses on release dates for their student body as opposed to, first come, first serve, even after me only needing a few points to have a G.E.D. awarded. I am completely auto-didacted.

Nonetheless, since I have written (3) books (Maurice: A Soul In Search of Itself, Freedom's Fight and Faith). A thesis in the psychology field, entitled; The Accumulation of Trauma Upon An African-American Male Within the Federal Bureau of Prisons (which I shared with a member of Congress). An excerpt in a summation written for a provision in the United Kingdom(UK), for at-risk youth, entitled; You Talk One on One(Your Overall Understanding of Talking and Linking Knowledge). And, founder of a start-up therapeutic dialogue re-entry group, here at F.C.I. Butner 2, entitled; Manhood 360: Individual and Cooperative Intervention.

Viktor E. Frankl(Concentration camp survivor), once wrote;

> "An active life serves the purpose of giving man the opportunity to realize values in creative work, while a passive life of enjoyment affords him the opportunity to obtain fulfillment in experiencing beauty, art,

or nature. But there is also purpose in that life which is almost barren of both creation and enjoyment and which admits of but one possibility of high moral behavior: Namely, a man's attitude to his existence, an existence restricted by external forces. A creative life and a life of enjoyment are banned to him. But not only creativeness and enjoyment are meaningful. If there is a meaning in life at all, then there must be a meaning in suffering. Suffering is an ineradicable part of life, even as fate and death. Without suffering and death, human life cannot be complete.

Physical/Health

In 2013 after a routine chronic care doctor's appointment for hypertension and hyperthyroidism, which I've been battling since 2005, I needed further evaluating because of a constant series of chest pains. The results concluded that I had coronary artery disease, that included (3) severely blocked arteries. In January of 2014, I underwent a triple by-pass open heart surgery at Monongalia General Hospital in Morgantown, West Virginia. I was 42 years of age.

Although I have been clean for over (8) years now, the addiction to heroin had came and went with a price. Physically, I now must ingest (6) different medications a day, for the rest of my life to balance illness preventability and disease stability. Spiritually, I lost both my parents to this drug. My father to an overdose. My mother, from complications related to the H.I.V. Syndrome, contracted through injected drug use.

The singer Lena Horne once said;

"It's not the load that breaks you down, it's the way you carry it."

<u>In Conclusion</u>

Your Honor, I believe that truth can be observed without a single word uttered or written. I believe that our hearts dictate a chronological order of movements in our lives, unconscious to even ourselves. As I know today that I am incarcerated on account of the dictations of my previous heart. An excessive imbalance of my 'bad side'. Though the carnage that I've left in the wake to enter this point of my life is yet and still inexcusable, therefor I could only seek mercy. In the most humbling entreaty and respect for the lives of my countrymen, I submit that; I am now ready to rejoin and build our society. To protect and nurture the lives therein. To be the man that I was meant to be that my family and community meant for me to be. Even so, the citizen that you want me to be, because you never sentenced me to the ultimate. Those words were not presented. Your Honor, in fairness, sentenced me to change… and, I did. I have accepted suffering appropriately and embarked on a lifetime journey of remorsefulness.

Saint Dominic once wrote;

"There is a need to overcome yourself. Expect this. If you work in the spirit of obedience to God's will and not your own, it will become easier and easier to overcome yourself and you will move closer and closer to the heart of your God. The closer you come to him, the less you struggle with self-will. The closer you come to him, the less you consider how the world is viewing you. Be content to be small in your spiritual life. Humility comes from an awareness of one's flaws and humility is necessity in your vocation. God is great and you are willing. This is how you are to proceed."

Sincerely,

Maurice W. Tyree

* * *

Mr. Maurice W. Tyree was convicted by Judge Robert I. Richter of first-degree premeditated murder, along with other offenses, on June 25, 2003, in the Superior Court of the District of Columbia. The sentence given was thirty-five years to life. As Mr. Tyree notes in the above Compassionate Release Letter to the presiding judge, Richter "never sentenced me to the ultimate." The death penalty was off the table. Tyree pled not-guilty, as advised by his counsel, even though there may have been a slight chance he would have received a more lenient sentence had he pled guilty.

By the time Mr. Tyree submitted this plea motion to the judge, almost 20 years after his conviction, Richter had retired. The letter was instead forwarded to the presiding judge at the time, Rainey Ransom Brandt, Associate Judge on the Superior Court of the District of Columbia. Brandt ultimately granted Tyree's release. This decision was far from a given, and no one can be sure if the letter he wrote contributed positively or not. In fact, there are many in the legal field who recommend against defendants writing these sorts of letters. Sometimes they end up having an "adverse effect," Tyree explained. Whatever the case may be, Mr. Tyree was eventually released on July 12, 2021.

(Not) the beginning

Maurice was not what one would call a 'career criminal.' Until the moment he found himself standing in front of Judge Richter, in fact, Maurice had only been briefly incarcerated once. At age fourteen, attempting to protect his friend, he shot at a man with a 22-caliber handgun. Although convicted of assault with a dangerous weapon and attempted murder, because of his age he served approximately two weeks and was let out on probation. The presiding judge at the time commented on Maurice's clean record, and how "he was trying to do the right thing" with his life. A judge noting that a fourteen-year-old has a clean record may provide some insight into what was expected of young people like Maurice.

Thirteen years later, when Judge Richter said, "Mr. Tyree I believe that you have a good side to you… however, you also have this bad side as well…", Maurice was taken aback. It was "like he threw water in my face", Maurice explained to me. Until that moment, he had not really considered himself – or the activities he engaged in – as exceptionally "bad". This may be difficult for some to understand but, simply put, environment shapes us. What we are surrounded with is what we accept as "normal", according to Maurice. In the world in which he grew up, engaging in certain behaviors in order to thrive – or simply to survive – was the norm.

Maurice explains that selling drugs was often just a way to take care of one's family, a "good" thing essentially. So if someone were to attempt to rob your business, your "drug store," then you would do what was necessary in order to protect your family's future. Thoughts of who you might be hurting, how someone else's family might instead be affected, does not necessarily enter into the equation. It is a "sick contradiction", concedes Maurice.

A human condition

It should be noted early on that this book will not be about the act that sent Maurice to prison. While there are various legal reasons to avoid going into detail about the situation, he argues that there is an even more important issue at hand. In the forefront, for him, is the issue of mental illness, a consistent cause and/or result of incarceration. This is a crucial factor, and a distinct disconnection for many outsiders' reactions to the incarcerated. People who have no idea of the circumstances inside are making decisions, literature, and policy based upon a gross lack of knowledge. That is something this book hopes to alleviate.

Maurice contends that along with self-education must come processing. It is not enough to take the time to learn what it might be like to live inside, one must also take the time to process that information, to process the feelings around that imagining. After all, it is uncomfortable to think too long about what it is we are really talking about when we discuss institutions designed to lock up human beings in cages. But if reform is to be enacted – and that is the hope here – then we must be willing to leave the true-crime drama stuff behind and contend with the personalization of the criminal. Maurice believes it is necessary to understand his crime through an illustration of his humanity. This is not to make excuses, nor garner pity. As Maurice says, he was wrong in doing what he did, "humanistically wrong." But the story is more than the crime.

As an illustration, Maurice references the book *Better, Not Bitter: Living on Purpose in the Pursuit of Racial Justice* by Yusef Salaam, one of the Exonerated Five. In his book, Salaam also chooses to circumvent any great detail of that day in New York's Central Park, which sent him and four others to prison for six years. Salaam writes, "To be clear, my story does not begin with the Central Park jogger case… And just as my story doesn't begin with the Central Park Five trial, it doesn't end with the exoneration…."[1]

In reading Salaam's book, Maurice observed that the writer's 'strategy' was such that the reader "didn't care about those details" of the alleged crime because they were compelled by a bigger story, a human's story. That is how he imagines this book to be received as well.

Not somewhere you want to be

Included in this very straightforward letter written for the Judge, Maurice references his addiction to heroin. This was something that began only once he was incarcerated. Awaiting his sentencing hearing, he was placed in solitary confinement at the Washington D.C. Central Detention Facility. During his time there, he was shuttled back and forth from courthouse to prison, awaiting sentencing and leaning on his Christian faith for support.

In the D.C. Detention Facility's "hole", while awaiting sentencing, Maurice befriended a prisoner on the other side of the wall. Despite not being able to see each other, they held long conversations about religion and the Bible, which provided much-needed encouragement for Maurice. One day, the man offered that he had something "to help him out." Maurice was eager, assuming it would be in the form of an especially pertinent scripture, or perhaps a new theological concept. A Bible was then slid under his door, wherein he was directed to open the book to a particular page. There he found, not a highlighted Bible verse, but a packet of white powder. Heroin. He had never used hard drugs before, but he was feeling incredibly desperate for some relief from the circumstances that he found himself in. At that moment, he truly felt he had "no more answers". He writes about this moment in a letter to one of the Inside-Out Prison Exchange program instructors. The letter appears in Chapter Five of this book, dated December 5, 2013.

So he tried the dope, even though that was not really how Maurice operated. Never one for "foreign stuff," he had not been an experimenter, largely in part because he was the one to discover his father dead of a drug overdose in his own home. But the isolation of solitary was getting to him and, as humans do when faced with crisis, he began to rationalize that even if he died from the drugs, at least he would get to see his father in the afterlife. And so, the using began. Maurice went from snorting the powder to injecting the drug into his veins. And, in case the reader is wondering, it was not all that difficult to secure drugs in prison. Maurice was able to sustain his habit for the next ten years.

Apparently, it is common knowledge inside that accessing drugs is fairly easy. Keri Blakinger is a criminal justice reporter who previously served two years for possession of heroin. Blakinger was recently interviewed about her new book, a memoir called *Corrections in ink*. She said, "Prisons are drenched with drugs. When I got to prison, I had someone who in the first week told me they could get me heroin and a needle if I wanted."[2]

In all, Maurice would serve time in four different carceral institutions. Once sentenced in Washington, he was sent to the United States Penitentiary, Big Sandy, in Kentucky – a high- security United States federal prison. After eight and a half years, for medical reasons, Maurice was moved to the United States Penitentiary, Hazelton, in West Virginia – another high-security federal prison. It was here that he began his participation in the Inside-Out Prison Exchange Program, an international education initiative involving, as their website reads, people from "both sides of the prison wall studying together through dialogue." Maurice continued these studies even after his release. It was also at Hazelton that Maurice received triple bypass surgery.

Due to his ongoing medical issues, Maurice was next sent to the Federal Correctional Institution (FCI) Butner Medium II in North Carolina, which is a medium security facility. Butner was known as one of the 'medical prisons'. This meant there was better care there and a little less chaos. It also meant it was a place where many inmates went to die, to see out their lives if they had no chance of parole or were terminally ill. There was "death every day", according to Maurice. But, in all of it, he was somehow not worried. After almost 20 years in prison, he felt sure that Butner was the place from where he would be released. He saw himself going home from there and he was correct in that vision.

But years before, early on in his incarceration, Maurice was not a hopeful man. He continued his drug use for years, until one day he simply found he'd had enough. For one thing, he was tired of all the effort it took just to hide the stuff, to duck the guards, to play "cat and mouse" all day, every day. The prison's random drug tests had him bloating himself with water for two hours ahead of time, attempting to eliminate any traces of the drug. At some point, he was pretty sure that prison staff knew he was an addict but he wondered if maybe they were just keeping it to themselves, until they could use it against him as a bargaining chip or for blackmail of some kind. He was hitting bottom, "feeling stagnated… like I preferred to die", even overdosing one time. So he just stopped – in one night. He remembers being on his bunk, talking to his cellie (cellmate) on the bunk above him. Sitting there with the needle and drugs in hand, he shared with his bunkmate how tired he was of it all. He believes God spoke to him in that moment, saying he would never get out of that prison if he kept using. Maurice decided he was not ready to accept that fate, that he could not see himself dying in a prison hospital. He declared to his cellie that he was through and flushed the binky (homemade syringe made from a ballpoint pen) and drugs down the toilet.

The effort of conversion

As Maurice explains it, this moment was not exactly a revelation. At the same time that he was feeling so despondent, he had also been experiencing a strange accumulation of confidence. He attributes this to the reading and writing practice that he had begun. While he spent a lot of that study time high, it began to occur to him that he might not "need" drugs anymore. He had thoughts to entertain and distract him now, questions that appeared the more he read, ideas that made themselves known to him in his own writing. His mind was lighting up and he wanted to make sure he was around to experience the intellectual, philosophical, and creative growth spurt that was occurring. Heroin was getting in the way of all that.

This attention to and desire for intellectual growth was not exactly surprising. While Maurice would not describe himself as an especially committed student in his youth, he does recall that many teachers remarked upon his intelligence. However, when he was told he was smart, it was typically attached to success on tests. The understanding was that if one did well on a test, then one moved on. It was all about moving on. There was nothing sustainable, nothing nurtured in that process. In fact, Maurice believes that part of what is hurting his community today is that lack of nurturing around young people's passions and, instead, overemphasis on tests and grades. He is not alone in that thinking, of course.

Once Maurice began reading in prison, he "began to travel", as he put it. Many of us have had this same experience, wrapped up in what we are reading – so much so that we feel as if we are there, with the writer and the writing. It was an act of escape for Maurice, taking him out of his circumstances – and sometimes his head – into other places entirely. Just "like doing drugs", it was "a release" that made him feel good, he says. It also made him feel hopeful, though not optimistic, as he – along with many scholars and philosophers – differentiates. Maurice had never had these feelings before and he ultimately became "addicted to hope". Or, as he writes in the release letter, "I fell yet again into another habit". This new habit was one of self-education and transformation.

Teaching and learning

Education is a complicated term, one that carries a very singular meaning for many people. In referencing Ta-Nehisi Coates' book, *Between the World and Me*, Maurice explains that, like Coates, he was never much of a classroom person, even as he had definitely become a book person. Coates writes: "The pursuit of knowing was freedom to me, the right to declare your own curiosities and follow them through all manner of books. I was made for the library, not the classroom. The classroom was a jail of other people's interests."[3] That is a statement others may also relate to.

There were classrooms in prison, too. And although the Prison Education Department offered a GED (General Education Development) program, Maurice did not avail himself of the opportunity. This turned out to be a sticking point for Judge Brandt in 2020 when reviewing Maurice's release motion. Through a letter to his lawyer, the judge questioned Maurice's commitment to reform, citing this lack of certification: "he has been incarcerated for almost 20 years, yet Mr. Tyree has no GED." The judge characterized Maurice's explanation regarding these circumstances as "hard to believe", calling into question his honesty. (See excerpt of letter below).

In fact, this judge seemed to be adamantly opposed to Maurice's release. She focused on his education status, calling "what is missing" in his educational file "most telling." Maurice's lawyer tried to assuage the judge's concerns around education by arguing that his client suffered from a kind of learning disability that hindered him from learning in a formal classroom environment. The judge responded to this explanation by saying it "makes no sense." A case manager also tried to persuade the judge as to what rehabilitation looked like in a prisoner – and the very real reasons why one inmate might sign up for one educational class but not another. The case manager testified that Maurice's rehabilitation was, in actuality, "impeccable".

The judge also argued that the "violent nature" of Maurice's initial offense, "disciplinary infractions" once inside, and "failure to comply with probation conditions", were indications that he may well still be a "danger to the community". All of these issues had already been addressed by Maurice and his lawyer. The infractions consisted of the two times he was found to mitigate his anger issues. However, according to his educational file, since 2018, Mr. Tyree has only completed 3 courses: two in 2018 and one in 2019.

Perhaps the most telling aspect of Mr. Tyree's educational file is what is missing. He has been incarcerated for almost 20 years, yet Mr. Tyree has no GED. Mr. Tyree defends that point by stating in a letter he wrote to Judge Richter that the Federal Bureau of Prisons prioritizes GED classes according to release dates. The Court finds that hard to believe considering Mr. Tyree has certificates from numerous other courses some of which, applying his above noted rationale, should have also been offered to those who have earlier release dates before him. It simply makes no sense.

While Mr. Tyree continues to make strides towards rehabilitation, the Court cannot conclude that the record demonstrates overall that Mr. Tyree no longer presents a danger to the community based on his criminal history, the violent nature of the instant offense, his disciplinary infractions and his demonstrated failure to comply with probation conditions.

The Court must also take into consideration that the decedent's mother, Grace Taylor, opposes Mr. Tyree's release. She has expressed that he should serve the "full time" of his sentence. She further stated, "My son is dead and is not able to come back, so why should the defendant get released early?" These remarks are salient because they re-focus us on the meaning behind the statute. In structuring this emergency legislation for felons, the city council put public safety first in the court's consideration for release. That was not by accident because even the city council understood that the Covid-19 health crisis could not become a "get out of jail free card." Mr. Tyree has strong familial support, however that support was present in his life throughout his criminal history.[14]

---

[14] *Id.* at 9-12 (citations omitted).

Figure 1. Excerpt of letter from Rainey Ransom Brandt, Associate Judge on the Superior Court of the District of Columbia

have a knife in his cell. This may have been against the rules, but it was not unusual as self-defense was a daily concern for prisoners. Maurice just simply got found out. The reference to the probation issue went back to his initial crime many years prior, in that he temporarily went on the run. He had previously been on probation for drug possession, so this was certainly a non-compliant act. These accusations were both accurate and old news.

When things do not align in the way that we expect, this can often lead to frustration and confusion. It is possible that the judge could not reconcile, for example, that the person who wrote that articulate, insightful, intelligent letter was also that same someone who was without any formal education. The tone of her response felt angry, almost resentful at times. Maurice may not have been compelled by that "jail of other people's interests", but he had educated himself exceptionally well on the things that mattered to him once he was in prison. One of the many books that provided him with major inspiration, was George Jackson's *Soledad Brother*. Jackson, a member of the Black Panther Party, served his time inside Soledad Prison, in California, between 1964 and 1970 constantly writing letters to everyone, from his mother to his lawyer to his comrades. As with Maurice, Jackson's letters sound as if they are written by a formally educated thinker, yet he did not graduate high school either. Jackson's book was a good part of the impetus behind Maurice writing the numerous letters included in this book.

George Jackson had issues with classroom education as well. But he also understood, at one point during his incarceration, that his requested release on parole would be predicated upon his finishing high school inside. Jackson attempted to be "a good boy", as he put it, making his way through the basic classes, until he got to a history class taught by an exceptionally patriotic instructor. In fact, according to Jackson, this teacher was so loyal to the U.S. that he taught a history highlighting the inferiority of every other nation on the planet in comparison to the United States. Jackson tried numerous times to switch out of the class, keeping his mouth shut for a full month. But then, one day, the teacher finished a lecture on corporations in America and asked:, "Now haven't we all the right to be proud?" Jackson could remain silent no longer. He replied, "No". A long conversation between teacher and student ensued. Jackson writes in a 1970 letter to his lawyer: "I got out of class that night, I haven't been able to get out of the joint, however".[4] Suffice it to say that education can look like a lot of things. For Maurice, "listening and reading" was his schooling of choice.

Education is what Maurice is attempting to offer in this book, as well. He notes that while prison happened to be "transformative" for him, it typically destroys most people. It attacks all aspects of one's humanity, the injuries to one's mental health being most serious. At the end of his letter to the judge, Maurice references a thesis he wrote titled: "The Accumulation of Trauma Upon an African-American Male, Within the Federal Bureau of Prisons". This essay appears at the end of this book. Suffice it to say, for now, that it is a serious and well-thought-out treatise on the damages inflicted to the human psyche when one is held behind bars. As stated, Maurice sent this piece to a congressperson, Representative Eleanor Holmes Norton, delegate to the United States House of Representatives for the District of

NATIONAL ASSOCIATION FOR THE ADVANCEMENT OF COLORED PEOPLE
4805 MT. HOPE DRIVE • BALTIMORE, MD 21215-3297 • (410) 580-5777

DERRICK JOHNSON
President & Chief Executive Officer

LEON W. RUSSELL
Chairman, National Board of Directors

OFFICE OF THE GENERAL COUNSEL

August 9, 2018

Maurice W. Tyree
Register #33159-007
Federal Correctional Institution
P.O. Box 1500
Butner, North Carolina 27509

Dear Mr. Tyree,

    Your letter has been received and reviewed by the NAACP Legal Department. We apologize for the delay in responding to your concern regarding the failures of the federal prison system.

    Your letter indicates that you are truly concerned about the effects of the prison system on African Americans.

    Please know that the concerns expressed in your letter are noted and we thank you for sharing them with us.

    The NAACP appreciates your vote of confidence.

                      Very truly yours,

                       The NAACP Legal Department

/AKB

www.naacp.org

Figure 2. Response letter from NAACP to Mr. Tyree

Columbia. He received a formal letter in response thanking him for his thoughts.

Maurice also forwarded the essay to the National Association for the Advancement of Colored People (NAACP) and federal justice department. At some point, the Department of Veterans Affairs also received a copy – in addition or instead of the intended recipients, he is not sure. The gist of this letter, which he wrote to accompany the essay, was that he was seeking help for his fellow prisoners.

While they all may have "messed up" at one point, he argues that the fact that no one on the outside seemed eager to fix the broken prison system only added to the burdens already borne by the incarcerated. Prison, he points out, is not typically a place for rehabilitation. Yet a lot of people act as if that is the intention. Maurice has some ideas on how things could change and believes that he can even teach those in power how to implement that change.

Maurice made connections as far as the United Kingdom, attempting to get his message across far and wide. While in prison, he availed himself of internet access – a service he paid for himself through a third-party vendor. In sharing his essays and poems widely, he ended up making contact with a social worker in the UK. She had started her own organization counseling families and youth, and was interested in Maurice's point of view and experience. She ended up including some of his writing in her promotional materials. We will hear a bit more about her later on in the book. Soon there were people from across the globe educating themselves on the human experience of incarceration, through his writing.

In keeping with his quest to address the mental health issues of incarcerated people, Maurice founded a therapy group at Butner prison. While he is a man who prefers to be "in the shadows", the process of putting the therapy group together made him feel something special, as if following a calling. While it is widely known, these days especially, just how hard it is to challenge people's belief systems, Maurice found he was able to bring divergent groups to the table for discussion. This would be no ordinary talk-therapy group either. He had in mind a kind of training session, wherein the older men inside would learn to counsel the younger men. The mission: to teach them to be grown men – but from where they were already, as opposed to forcing some one-size-fits-all rendition of manhood upon them.

Manhood means something different to different people, according to Maurice. Thus, the curriculum would be tailored to each young man in question and the organization was to consist of layers of mentorship. Each youth would have an appointed personal mentor and then that mentor would in turn have a facilitator. Maurice would be the lead, overseeing the facilitators, mentors, and youth. This was his (intentionally) intersectional approach to mental health care. Unfortunately, as with so many plans during the pandemic, the program was shut down just as it was ready to launch.

Organizing such a group, maneuvering through the bureaucratic red tape of Federal Corrections, was no small task. There were so many ideologies, which he differentiates from the diverse personalities he also contended with. The experience of being in the role of a teacher and mentor, as he organized the group, gave him confidence that he could navigate any system. He intends to utilize the experience and knowledge gained during those final years on the inside to implement similar programs in his own community, now that he is on the outside.

The end of one chapter

In the judge's response letter to Maurice's Compassionate Release Plea, she characterizes the views of his victim's mother as "salient". This kind of statement made it seem she had already made her decision. The mother apparently called for Maurice to serve the full sentence as initially ordered, objecting to his early release due to COVID risks. The judge pointed to this as relevant, something she was taking into consideration alongside his low formal education status.

The attorney argued that there was no precedent for including, as evidence, the opinions of a victim's family. He also provided testimony from a medical doctor to Maurice's chronic illness, explaining in great detail how vulnerable he would be if there were to be a COVID outbreak in the prison.

The disconnect that Maurice has identified as one of the largest obstacles to prison reform and rehabilitation is quite evident in this situation. The judge really had no means of contextualizing her expectations with the reality of what actually goes on inside a prison. And, based upon all that Judge Brandt had stated in her letter, Maurice assumed he would be remaining in prison for many years to come. But ultimately the judge ruled in his favor, explaining at the appeal hearing that she was bound by law to let Maurice go free. His medical condition, in the face of a potential COVID outbreak within the prison, was a primary factor. She had no choice, she said. By the way, Maurice notes that he and the judge are "good" now.

This chapter sets the stage for the 20 years Maurice spent in prison. But instead of lurid violent crimes and dramatic courtroom scenes, people and their stories will be foregrounded. There are judges and cellmates, government officials and lawyers, cousins, lovers, and doctors. The main character, Mr. Maurice W. Tyree, is a man who started life in a difficult, yet somewhat ordinary, fashion. Through the personal letters he shares and narrates in the following chapters, it becomes clear that he has transformed himself into a poet, philosopher, and activist. But there are many more people broken than redeemed by their time spent in prison and that is what he wants us to learn. To that end, Maurice believes that first the reader must see him as a man, see those who are incarcerated as human beings. If that happens, then he has confidence it is "a given" that this book "will change somebody's life".

1
Fending for myself

September 2, 2010

Marquetta*,

In immense admiration of you and with an overwhelming state when graced with your correspondence, thanks for reaching out.

I must share a brief, yet sincere, revelation with you as acknowledgment is subsequent to application.

An ideal was planted in me between the months of August or September, 2005 when I was witnessing, via newspaper articles, and being informed of this while in solitary confinement, that a hurricane titled Katrina was ravaging the city of New Orleans and others in Louisiana and Mississippi. Though I understood perfectly that nothing could have prevented this massive storm from prevailing, nonetheless, during and after its' contact with people on the land, I saw that my people (humanity) had been left in a total state of helplessness. At that moment

I began to independently attempt to closely observe humanity, as well as the nature of the world and myself from a position of factual objectivity. As the entire world was watching in horror, people were suffering and dying and I was viewing horrific photos as if it was my very own kinship being tangled in this web of experience involving nature and man.

As I continued to review the conditions of that day's atrocities an intense, yet foreign, feeling came over me. Up until that point, nothing in my life's journey had taught me how to address this kind of emotion that I was feeling for complete strangers that resided so far away from my own domicile.

I wept and prayed for two days in remembrance of those people. I remember being plagued with anxiety simply because a mere emotion was all that I had to offer them. I told you to send the clothing and shoes, that I had left at your home prior to my incarceration, to the Red Cross as a token of our required duty in aiding and assisting with their recovery needs. I became extremely upset by the menial response that you gave me after my request.

Praying for the well being of those people wasn't the only thing that I petitioned the Creator for. Viewing what had occurred also made me ask the Creator to strengthen my ability to obtain divine understanding of what is the entirety of myself. I critically reasoned with myself about the conditions of the entire circumstance, which included the interaction among a multi-cultural mix of ethnicities and classes who were at the mercy of nature and themselves. This made me deeply desire to know the scientific method underlying societal balance which concerned the inhabitants of this world to whom I was now feeling an attachment to, at least from an ecological point of view.

Now I will turn this letter's focus to that which you had made reference to in your last correspondence. First, you should never entertain the notion that your thoughts to me are complaints. I understand how the heart and psyhce work in concordance together when trying to analyze eyents viewed through your own human propensities. Whatever can be offered from me will be without hesitation, and in compliance with love and respect.

I sense that you are concerned with your aging process. Your increase in age only means that the natural transformation that governs your (our) life is taking place. This can only be a hinderance if it doesn't transpire. Your unique experience in this life must move to its' next phase. The deterioration of the physical body, as you know, begins on the very same day that you are born. Beauty, though, lies in the fact that your mental and spiritual maturity continues to be confirmed the more elder you become.

In reference to what I previously expressed to you concerning and in accordance with dealing with my children's behavior, the fact of the matter is that the evolutionary process persists in everything. They should evolve in perfect harmony and made into great human beings as that process takes its' course. Nonetheless, we also can cause great limitations in their ability to exercise this greatness by not properly evolving ourselves. We must be careful, though, that our responsibility transcends beyond the obligations to our children. Among other things in this process is; the Earth, the community, and others of humanity. All must be given their proper measure in the evolutionary process so that each may qive balance to one another in this universal process.

Granted, my children do not understand, presently, how to open their hearts and minds to me. I must ask does this delay mean that I must cease in my duties and responsibilities to the rest of the process?

I Regard You Supreme,
Brother

*Author's eldest sister

I was writing to my sister about my feelings towards Hurricane Katrina, the deadly storm that washed over the city of New Orleans and surrounding areas in August 2005. At the time of the storm, I was in solitary confinement. I was sometimes able to access a newspaper, but I was pretty limited as to how much information I got. What I did know was that the storm was devastating – the images were so disturbing. It was something about that disaster, and its outcomes, that felt personal to me.

Like I said in the letter, looking back I saw that some kind of seed had been planted within me at the very moment of that hurricane. I just didn't know it at the time. I started to change. Seeing all those people attempting to survive, fending for themselves in dire circumstances; I saw myself. I was fending for my life, too, just in a different environment – and for different reasons. But I felt connected to the helpless humanity, battered by circumstances outside their control. I saw my life, and my fellow inmates' lives, in that storm. And I cried – for those both inside and outside of prison. I also cried at the new feeling I was experiencing, a compassion for strangers. I had not carried a lot of compassion with me early on in life; it had been every man for himself.

In this letter to Marquetta, I was finally able to articulate the ideas and emotions I had been having for some time. It was harder for me to say what I meant early on, for a few reasons – isolation and illiteracy most specifically. But after spending so many years educating myself in prison, intellectually and emotionally, I gained some tools to clarify to my sister just how transformational an event like Hurricane Katrina was for me.

And this is why I had to tell her how disappointed I was, even so many years later, that she had not honored my request to donate my belongings to the hurricane victims. How could she not understand that the people in New Orleans were more in need than some random family members wanting a particular sweater or pair of jeans? There was that disconnect, that impossibility of understanding by some people of how things were outside their own realm.

Maybe I had not been able to make it clear enough to my sister, at the time, just how important the act of donating was to me. But those five years later, in this letter, I tried again to explain what it was I was feeling when I made that request.

It was in this same letter that I also shared some of my thoughts on aging, but about philosophical aging, not chronological. It might sound like I was suggesting that at least Marquetta was able to age on the *outside*, free to care for her body and mind however she wanted. But that wasn't it. I was saying that staying young forever makes no sense. Why would someone beat themselves up regarding the inevitably of aging, I wondered. After all, an increase in age is only a hindrance if it doesn't transpire, as far as I could see. Like they say, getting old is better than the alternative.

This had not always been my line of reasoning. But I relearned life in prison, so my perspective changed a lot. Before being incarcerated, I might have even seen my sister's point, and related with her on the perils of aging. But those would have all been lies when it came to what she wanted to hear regarding the subjects of beauty and longevity. But after all I had been through, and all I had learned, I could no longer say anything that wasn't true to me. That caused a lot of distance between me, my sister, and other family and friends, too. People don't want unapologetic speaking, especially when it is unexpected, coming from someone who used to be a very different person.

Oct 5, 2010

[Behind the scene]

It took me quite a long time to realize, then to admit openly, that my mother, father, and I were an alienated link from the moment I was born. Today I can honestly say that I truly never knew them, nor, did they truly wanted to know me. So I assumed.

I never resided with either of them for a lengthy period of time. The time that I did however, my mother, broke my bones and mentally tormented me so often and severely that, to date, my emotional and spiritual predictability is yet and still insummarizeable. My father, though minus the physical contortion, simply ignored me and the nurturing process altogether. It wasn't until the final moments of their life on this earth when a bizarre twist of affairs led me to understand everything in which they could not express while they lived. They chose me to be the very last person that they would make amends with before the departure. Within a couple of minutes these two wonderful human beings summed up many of years of love and honor for their son.

October 5, 2010

Teresa*,

May this letter find your mind idled in a state of tranquility and your loving spirit aligned with that of your youngest descendant.

First, I must express that I miss you and love you with authority. Secondly, if there are any misconceptions concerning the contents of my letters to you I truly forward my deepest apologies for such. You are, however fully aware that I mean no disrespect in this matter. I have never, considering our relations position, intentionally or maliciously injected a portion of disrespect into this relationship. The force that I propel, at times, in bluntness and, perhaps with an appearance of insensitivity, merely comes from the long and tedious years I have spent conjuring up the actual understandings of who I am, What I am, and the synonymous action that is part of both of them. My apologies are sincere, though, I do not regret for whom I've become and to what I am striving so hard to be.

Lately, I have been pondering on the true meaning of what is a mother. I've partially concluded that it is far more defined than a place where a fetus is conceived or from where a baby is abstracted from the female's womb.

What will the child become without the lessons taught by the mother? Is the child the rightful creditor or discreditor of a mother's legacy?

While I shall further the reasoning in my reflecting, concerning motherhood, I must first ask you to answer these two questions.

I bid your enlightenment.

                                      Please be well,
                                                        Son

* Author's biological mother

Teresa was my biological mother. I was raised mostly by my grandmother, who I really saw as mom. Sometimes I would call Teresa *mother*, but other times I called her by her name – that usually occurred after one of our angry moments. She would do the same to me, playing the name game depending on how she felt about me, and what I had done for her. Teresa was destructive (and unapologetic about it) due to circumstances outside her control. But the choices she made around those circumstances always made things worse, such that I was on my own as a child a lot of the time.

The questions that I ask Teresa at the end of this letter were meant to be provocative as much as anything else. "What will the child become without the lessons taught by the mother?" and "is the child the rightful creditor or discreditor of a mother's legacy?" was just my way of asking her to think more deeply. I had begun this new way of communicating, a fresh approach to sharing my thoughts and feelings. I thought maybe this change would be the thing that somehow reached across our divide that had been there since my earliest years. After all, there is always something in children that retains a spark of hope for parental love and acceptance, even if they haven't yet experienced it. I guess I thought there was some slim chance for clarity between son and mother because I had done so much mental processing of my own in prison.

But Teresa never answered those questions I asked, and we never did cross that divide.

```
February 5, 2011

Wanda*,

Greetings. May the Creator's might move
your yearning spirit as it does the Earth
itself. For there is where true peace is
bred. Peace as being a state of mind, as is
loneliness that is induced by the health of
the spirit.

The emotion from loneliness enters the
equation because we as human beings still
require the interdependency we share with
other human beings. You can make the health
of your spirit strong by first understanding
and implementing your role within the cycle
```

of the universe. It is my humble opinion that we learn to love not merely by tongue, but through expression that is complimentary, honoring, building with, caring for, educating, nurturing, respecting, admiring, and protective of one another which a family of people should, and must, do. When we do so, we begin to bridge the gap across which is found pain, ruin, isolation, suffering, broken homes, self denial, and genocide all of which our people have endured in the aftermath of our ancestor's version of enslavement.

You must feel empowered. You have procreated and also helped to create strength in the mental and spiritual life that is contained in.the children that you have produced, You have been, and are, an unparalleled liaison in this creative process. You should be empowered by your role and not beat yourself down because your counterpart has yet to uphold his responsibility in this process that follows sexual intercourse. If there has not yet come a counterpart that is willing to compliment you in this process it is simply not your misery to retain.

You are truly special within your womanhood. Your answers to my questions touched the core of my humanness. As the comrade George

Jackson once quoted: "Fortune must soon smile on you, because sincere effort is always rewarded." The last three questions could have only been answered in theory, because I already see the answers embodied in you. I just wanted yorir personal definition of that which I can already observe. You truly embody the definition. Fried Chicken though? You have to come a little more original than that. That's the favorite food of everyone in the neighborhood. Tell Maddi that I send my love and that she shares a birthday in the same week as her cousin, Le'mia. Tell Morgan That I send my love and that her birthday is on the same exact day as Maurice Jr., her other cousin. Tell Mya that I send my love as well and, with her permission, I would love to correspond with her more regularly.

As for the answering of your question: Am I all right? In reference to my physical health I have a slight case of ypertension", which sometimes gives me headaches. However, I believe that I will be fine. In reference to my spiritual and mental health, I have not been this focused in my entire existence. No ineffectual degree of ignorance can disturb what I've obtained in wisdom at this particular point in my life. I've arrived

```
at this junction by following, in depth,
the first two laws of nature which are the
law of motion and the law of order.

I love you, my beloved sister, and my nieces
to an extreme.

Please stay well. I disembark by declaring
my allegiance to· your well being.

                                    Love,
                                    Maurice

* Author's sister
```

Man, woman, family

In the letter to my sister, Wanda, I was trying to lift her up, remind her of her successes. I wanted her to see that she was a woman who deserved a decent partner in her life, that she shouldn't settle for less. That's what I meant when I wrote: "If there has not yet come a counterpart that is willing to compliment you in this process it is simply not your misery to retain." Just keep on walkin', is all I was trying to say.

I have very strong feelings on this subject because, over the years, I have come to a better understanding of a woman's perspective. As in, it's his loss if a man cannot prove himself worthy of a worthy woman. This was what moved me to start organizing that young men's counseling group that is referenced in the Introduction. I believe – really, I *know* – these lessons are not being taught enough, and I feel qualified to speak on the subject as a person who has lived both sides. There's no need for all these young men to keep on going without any support, like I did.

I wronged a lot of women in my young life; I undervalued them and our relationships. I have had many years to think about these actions and have finally started understanding why I was the way I was. I finally understood what the phrase, "hurt people hurt people" really means. I was hurt by my parents, in so many ways. So, in turn, I ended up perpetuating that cycle and hurting my own children – and their mothers, too. But that was a long time ago. And while it took many years, I do believe I now know the value of a partnership and just what kind of investment it takes to keep one going. My fiancée and I just got married and I am so glad for the opportunity to practice what I now understand is true commitment.

(Behind the scene)

LaKeisha's mother and my father were sister and brother. Her mother being the youngest of my paternal grandmother's (6) children while my father being the eldest, and both how since passed away from a drug overdose. LaKeisha and I grew up together under the guardianship of our grandmother, Shirley, also known as, Ma Smokey.

March 2, 2011

Lakeisha*,

May this scribe find you in the best of spiritual, mental, and physical health. On the basis of the message that you sent to me, via (FB), concerning our present mental state after the death of our impeccable mother (Grandmother), I will by-pass the formalities and get right to the point.

For me, the hardest part, mentally, was having to endure the grief that comes with such a spiritual loss without having the consolation that comes with having family by your side. This feeling was not simply for my own personal pacification, but was the first sign to rear its' existence that our family's unified identity was beginning to decline. This is upsetting to an extreme for me because our mother, through sound poverty, perpetuated during her entire lifetime the spirit and need for such unification. Her entire nature was to teach us these lessons. And we, without regard for those lessons betrayed their legacy within a matter of days of her death. In the beginning, my anger, confusion, and bitterness was aimed at that betrayal.

Our phenomenal mother shared her blood (sickness), sweat

(hustling to provide), tears (despair), and sacrifices (providing for you, I, and others long after her very own children were grown and on their own). She did this for generation after generation without a hint of regret or act of contempt. The strongest and most prevalent of her attributes was unconditional acceptance. Whether we were right, wrong, or indifferent to society or ourselves, she welcomed us with outstretched arms in the rhythm of love.

Your question to me is; How do you cope?

The most intense and realistic dream of my life occurred the day after I was informed of her death. She was speaking to me in the most commanding tone that I have ever heard in her voice. I was weeping during the entire time of this exchange. She said, "Teny? I'm gone now, and I will no longer be able to protect you. Now, it is you that I need. I need you to protect our family. I began to plead with her stating; "I can't. I have nothing, I don't know nothing, and I'm locked up!" She rebutted with; "Yes you can. You are the one and you are much stronger than that which you believe you are".

Now I cope very well indeed. After that night of revelation, I began to try prioritizing my strengths in accordance with that command. From that point forward my life started to feel more natural and simpler.

I cope by extending myself into the legacy that embodied the spirit of my mother's way of life. I cope but not allowing this connection to be disturbed by the selfishness of society. And, if there is such a thing as her looking down on me, I cope very well by knowing that she is full of joy watching my manhood take its' rightful place within the core of her heart and soul.

I have and will always view you as my endeared sister. I will always keep our kinship intact, even if I am left to do this simply in my heart. My family obligation has been commanded and, thereby, I must fulfill those duties.

Please join her and I on this intrepid expedition.

I Bid Your Collaboration,
Cousin

* Author's cousin

As I noted in the "Behind the Scenes" section, my cousin Lakeisha and I were more like siblings than cousins because we both did most of our growing up with my grandmother, Shirley. We also both lost a parent to drug addiction, so we mourned Shirley's death like we had lost our mother. In my letter, I'm trying to express how hard it was to mourn alone in prison, without any family around. My grandmother believed in family unity above all else, yet it was nowhere to be found in our own family at that moment.

Basically, those lessons on the importance of family, unity, and unconditional love were betrayed by my grandmother's own family, and that causes me great pain to think about. Instead of sticking together, we all isolated from each other, for all sorts of reasons. There has always been this conflict in my life, because of the way I was raised in that every-man-for-himself mentality. But when my cousin and I were essentially orphaned, my grandmother took us both in, no questions asked. That act of love went against everything I had been taught up until that point. And now, outside of prison, I continue to witness this conflict in my own family. My grandmother raised two young children who weren't her own in a small two-bedroom home, her door always open to those in need. At the same time, today I see some of my relations living in mansions who won't even bother to open their door to a brother or a cousin. Sometimes people get stuck on the idea of fending for themselves even when it's not necessary anymore.

The way I see it, this is a larger cultural problem. Like I notice the way partners speak to and about each other, their unwillingness sometimes to invest in each other. This is a sign of the times, an accumulation of all sorts of things. There is nothing like being out of society for 20 years to help you gain perspective on what society looks like. It's sort of like traveling to a new country – someone who was incarcerated for so long has an opportunity to see things that other people may have stopped noticing. Add to that some curiosity and a little intellectuality, and I find I have a lot to say about where we all are today. This makes some people uncomfortable. Like I said, people don't like unapologetic speaking. And that's pretty much all I have these days.

Co-author's note

Historically, the African American family has been attacked, assaulted, and disassembled by America's power structure. Maurice's grandmother was probably well aware of this. She took it upon herself to care for "generation after generation" of her family's children, perhaps, in order to make some sort of repair to the destruction leveled upon the Black family all these centuries. Late comedian and activist Dick Gregory observed that too often he heard Black people longing for the good old days, when family was family, ostensibly. But when would that have been for the African American, he asks? Was it "when white folks could just come in the house and lynch any n----- in the family they wanted…?" Or when Black fathers died fighting for their country in WWII yet, "the German who killed your Daddy can come to America and live and work where your Daddy can't work…?" No, he tells the audience, "This is family, right here…" as he points to the majority-Black audience in front of him.[1] Family is not always those with whom one shares blood ties; experience can be a bond unto itself.

Dick Gregory was illustrating the ways in which keeping a Black family together has been fraught with obstacles placed in the way by white supremacist systems. And this has been intentional. The prison industrial complex is just one of those systems designed to keep Black communities in chaos while taking advantage of continued cheap labor once slavery was abolished. And thus, as illustrated so aptly in Ava DuVernay's film, *13th*, the penal system was born. This institution continued the systemic abuse and isolation of Black people, especially men. The over-incarceration of Black men – so often a result of wholly inequitable jail sentences when compared to other races – has done much to tear at the fabric of the Black family.

In a 2016 interview with DuVernay in *The Atlantic,* she was asked if she had thought much about this connection between slavery, criminalization, and mass incarceration growing up. It turns out she did:

> I knew a lot of it. I grew up in Compton [central Los Angeles]. There was a heavy police presence growing up in the '80s, '90s in Compton. I'd see a cop and I didn't think safety, like my counterpart who didn't grow up in Compton. I'd think, "Oh boy, what are they coming for? And who are they coming after?" …Asking someone, "What are you doing this weekend?" "Oh, I'm going to see my father. He's locked up." Asking, "Hey, where's Derrick who lives up the street? I haven't seen him in a while." "Oh, he got locked up."
>
> Police officers coming to people's houses on my block. Cruisers going up the street, ghetto birds overhead…[2]

Maurice's grandmother, aka Ma Smokey, seemed to know all about this. As Dr. Joy DeGruy suggests, in originating the theory of Post Traumatic Slave Syndrome, there are historical reasons for the many adaptive behaviors of contemporary African Americans. The memories of abuse are embodied, DeGruy argues, and then heightened by the ongoing systemic racism of the present. In other words, people can recall ancestral experiences in a myriad of ways, and they will often react to those past memories through their present-day behavior. Maurice, for one, benefited from his grandmother's memory and the open-hearted nature that it created in her. At the same time, he mourned the ways in which he believed her legacy of family connection had been swept aside, as if they all went back to their proverbial corners after her death.

However, as is evident time and again, Maurice also found motivation in his troubles. After a visionary dream referenced in the letter to Lakeisha, he comes to a sort of peaceful determination that he will be the one to progress his grandmother's legacy, despite "the selfishness of society." We see in this collection of letters to loved ones and others one of the ways in which he follows through on this promise.

```
November 12, 2011

Marquetta,

May the terms within this synopsis suffice
as an unfeigned and strengthened renewal of
the radiant spectacle of our relationship.
There will be no more situations that will
prevent me from divulging my love and
admiration for you ever again.

The contemptuous E-mail, that I once sent
you, in which I tried, using defensive
tactics, to fend off the opinions of Mia and
yourself shall never be considered again. In
my amplified sense of understanding, I accept
my shamefulness and I am humbly apologetic
in every segment of the expression. Though,
we will employ disagreements in the future,
malicious intent will not take its' place
amongst our sound presentations.
```

You've disclosed the need to recoup after our conflict so that time could aid in your mental and spiritual health's harmony and I, as your kindred spirit, assumed the same requirement in this harmonious cycle.

I, in awe inspiring etiquette, have referred to you as my kindred spirit reflecting the fact that our connection is greater than the biological structure that forms our relationship. When you are happy I am relieved of a burden. When you are in pain it is felt long before I am informed of it. And, when I am responsible for your pain I have also afflicted myself with injury.

As I move forward in this letter to your essential dispositions concerning our immediate family members I must admit, in spite of their balanced self incriminations, that I still remain astonishly intrigued by them. Perhaps it is due to the studious observations which I've deployed concerning their distinctive personalities.

My methods not only give me the insight to engage them justly, but it also allows me to identify the superior deficiencies that propel their personalities to gouge the imprint of our family's identity. They, as well as I, have been subjected psychologically, socially, etc..... to so much in inconsistent reality and, as a result, they should be dealt with in a manner based on empathy and encouragement.

Send me a photo of the children at the church and yourself. Give Jada* a photo of me and send me one of her as well. Relay to her my admiration of her and my advocacy for her cause. If you hear from any of my extraordinary children tell them that I love them and will appreciate connecting with them as soon as possible.

It is in the truth in what was said that the practice of silent stillness brings the correct answers and, universal guidance.

I Bid You Credence,

Brother

* Mentally challenged child from sister's church mentoring program.

A father's role

Marquetta and I had a complicated relationship. I felt very close to her in a lot of ways, so I communicated with her directly. I mean I didn't use that filter most people do when discussing intense issues. The "contemptuous email" I reference in this letter was one of those times my filter was not in use. I cussed her out but then I regretted it. I don't even recall what it was that got me so mad, only that it had something to do with how she talked to my daughter, Le'mia. I felt she crossed some boundaries. Even though in prison I was still the father, and I believed in showing children respect, even while teaching them the ways of the world. That was something I didn't see much of growing up, and I wanted my kids to have a different experience.

It is not easy to parent from prison. You don't really know what your children are doing, especially if phone calls, letters, and visits are few and far between.[3] And that was the case for me and my children, my Reasons. The children spent a lot of time with my sister, Marquetta, while I was in prison. And although I am grateful for that family tie, I was still angry that I wasn't the one raising my kids. I had forced them to spend their young lives fending for themselves. It was my fault that I was not available, but it was society's, too. I see it as a 50/50 share of responsibility.

I was taken away from my children by society, not just through the penal system, but by society at large. Where I was raised, and how I was raised, has a lot to do with the sickness of this country. I do hold society accountable for the ways the cards are stacked against people like me; people whose parents have been broken by society themselves, people who grow up in neighborhoods where poverty is everywhere and crime seems the only response, and for people whose educational experience is old books, angry teachers, and violence.

Co-author's note:

There are many publications produced around this issue of parenting from prison. Themes of remaining hopeful, assuring children they are not responsible for their parent's situation and accepting that the children's feelings are at the forefront. In fact, the guidelines are similar to those provided to parents who are recovering addicts who are parents in their own right, but have been absent – emotionally if not also physically – from their children. However, few of the authors of the aforementioned publications have actually experienced incarceration themselves. This is evident in the ordered nature of some of the instructions parenting, an order that does not jibe with a typical day in the life of a prisoner.

One publication stands out however, from *The Marshall Project*. "Nonprofit journalism about criminal justice", *The Marshall Project* features writing by those with personal experience in the criminal justice system. In one essay, incarcerated writer Demetrius Buckley offers an illustration of both the messiness of parenting from behind bars but also the possibilities: "On our calls, my 11-year-old cracks jokes, laughs at mine, and generally keeps me on my toes. But I'm also learning things about her that require me to be even more present. That's difficult to do when you're serving time in maximum security prison."[4]

Ryan Moser, also incarcerated at the time, wrote about his son:

> It was selfish to get arrested and leave him to fend for himself, an unthinkable act of abandonment that hurt him to the core. I know this because he told me. He told me with unanswered letters and when he ignored my videograms. He told me with curses typed in emails expressing anger at a deadbeat dad who chose drugs over his son. He told me with the yearlong silence that followed those emails. The hardship of serving time in prison paled in comparison to the existential crisis of missing my child growing older.[5]

January 8, 2012

Marquetta,

Greetings my beloved sister. I must explain and apologize for my correspondence, both past and future, with the nature of their contents being accepted as very technical. How does one suppress or disembody that which he is thinking? I can only suggest that it would be the same as telling an individual that upholds a Christ like mind, not to demonstrate in their actions, what their mind is upholding. So, my beloved sister, I must invoke an apology because the fact is that I will continue to live out what is within the cosmos of my mind.

I wish we could sit before one another and converse for many hours at a time. We have the ability, you and I, to elaborate in depth about a variety of subject matters. I have given you the rights to my thoughts which are sacred, in their entirety, to me. Finding someone who is genuine in character is almost non-existent and the requirement to sooth the mind through healthy interactions becomes a creed of normality.

Now as things stand in the new light of different days, I have noticed in your previous correspondence, where it concerns the family's behavior (especially Mom's), that you spend the most energy preserving their symptoms. You pay very little attention as to why they have become behaviorally imbalanced and what are the cures for these imbalances. When viewed as a whole this shows, perhaps, an ineffective observation on the part of the one who is concerned. Without being too technical about this we must seize, in these reflective opportunities, the appropriate overview remedies that will us to diagnose our kin with the intent to comfort their well being and preserve their humanity.

In conclusion, the book writing idea has been proposed to me on a few occasions. In terms of time and the development of the exact academic necessities, it may be considerably simplistic. However, if one should possess the unique quality of producing projects under the literary arts banner, my opinion is that it should be the artist's intention to seek some form of liberation within the reader's mentality. A great effort to understand people in general must be made in order to identify their circumstances and conditions. For example; the African-American people. First, the origins of their African identity will have to be understood. Second, the same will have to occur concerning their American origins, so that there can be a full evaluation of their behaviors and conditions. In this the literary agent can exercise sound logical reasoning that will boast good writing material. Therefore, there will be much to learn and consider before I can integrate you into the world of literary arts.

Inform your child that I've inquired about her, and I'm corresponding. Let my Jr. know that I am requesting updated photos of Keari and, did Ms. Lakeisha receive my letter and Birthday cards for Keari?

Farewell,
Maurice

A changing mind

Even after disagreements and miscommunications, I always had the desire to share the cosmos of my mind with Marquetta. Yet, after being released and going to live with her, our differences created too much conflict. You can see some of these differences in the letters I write to her. I would ask her to consider expanding her perspectives on issues, think about religion differently, consider what humanity really is. These were things I thought and read and wrote about a lot in prison, and I was eager to share my new ideas with her and others. In the letter above I was asking Marquetta to consider not only the *results* of our parent's difficulties but also the *causes*. This is a reflection of the evolution of my thinking while incarcerated. I began to find that the typical human mind (like mine) was limited, and not useful in understanding and analyzing the bigger questions in life. I became fascinated with those bigger questions and exercised my brain into expansion. Around family, I often feel alone in this quest.

This change in my outlook created distance between me and the people that I had known – who had known me – before I went to prison. At this point, unfortunately, I am basically estranged from my two surviving sisters. Marquetta is no longer alive. My siblings feel like strangers to me after spending 20 years in prison, and I think I feel like a stranger to them, too. This is probably some sort of natural result of my situation, but it feels like no one really wants to try to get to know the "new" me.

I should say, they did not have a lot of preparation time. My release was pretty sudden for a system that usually moves so slowly. The combination of the COVID pandemic and my medical condition created an opportunity for me that I had not expected. And neither had my family. On the day of my release, I went to Marquetta's house, in Washington, DC. But the stay there was short. We were just not the same people anymore. I ended up transferring to a halfway house. You might wonder how bad things must be for a person who has been inside federal prison for 20 years to leave the comfort of a relative's home. The answer is: when the relative expects that person who was forced to leave their old life behind to spend a new life in prison will be the same person when they come out as when they went in.

I do understand why my family was looking for the old Maurice, responding to me the way they would have in the past, as if I was still that same man doing the same things. But I had worked hard during my years in prison to transform myself, and I was just not willing to return to the family dynamics of before. The new and improved Maurice was not someone to be bossed around, told what to do. I did not want the kind of advice that was being provided, because no one was asking me what *I* wanted or how *I* saw myself going forward. Their words were empty to me. I had a plan, if anyone had taken the time to ask, and it seemed a lot clearer than the ones these people on the outside had, far as I could see.

The controlling nature of the relationship with my sister really became triggering; she turned into the enemy in my eyes. Remember, I had been told what to do – and where to go and what to say, and even who I was – for the last two decades, by people who did not even acknowledge my humanity. Being around my sister felt too similar. The moment I moved out of my sister's and into the transitional home, I felt as if the weight of the world was off my shoulders. This might be hard to understand for someone who has never been incarcerated but that was my experience.

The question that continues to come up in my mind is why humans are so bad at stepping back and seeing someone from a fresh perspective. Even though most of us have been taught to think a certain way, it is possible to evolve that thinking. That is, I think, the point of our lives – to evolve. I should have been the slow one in my family, the one who was stagnant after all that time in one place, in isolation for so much of my time there. But I had spent those years in prison challenging my mind, and it felt as if I had progressed light-years. Meanwhile, my sister was still fussing about the same things she had always fussed about, even with all the freedom she had to evolve. None of this is all that surprising though, and I can't blame my sister completely for our differences. There's just nothing like forced isolation to get the mind working overtime.

Co-author's note

Imagine a monk's life for example, the amount of time and space they take to pray, to meditate, to ruminate. Most of them gain deeply spiritual connections with this world and beyond. In fact, some of the most iconic figures in history were in isolation, Maurice reminded me during one of our conversations. And he is correct. William Shakespeare wrote *King Lear* in quarantine from the bubonic plague; Mary Shelley wrote *Frankenstein* while on lockdown in Indonesia after a volcanic eruption; and of course, Dr. Martin Luther King, Jr. wrote his "Letter from Birmingham Jail" – often called the most important document of the Civil Rights Movement – while in prison. Loneliness can be both a burden and a blessing for some.

2
No more keeping it to myself

I was in a lot of unknowns during my time locked up, a good part of which was spent in isolation. If it had not been for this oppressive scenario, however, I am not so sure I would have succeeded in reprogramming myself. It was strenuous and I dug deep so that I could transform myself there, all within the conditions of the prison system. I think it might be too easy to keep up the status quo on the outside; regular people don't always believe they can change – or that they have to. I look back at the beginning of COVID for example, the way people on the outside acted so dramatically, like they were ready to hang themselves or something. It was like it was the first time in history they had been constrained by outside forces. But I was used to a life of constraint, even before prison. My perspective was different.

In the January 2012 letter to Marquetta, I mentioned a "book writing idea". What you are reading is basically the result of that idea. I wanted to "seek some form of liberation within the reader's mentality" because I knew that people's minds would need to be freed from a lot of preconceived notions. I wanted to encourage people to work hard to understand other people – people they didn't know but maybe still had opinions about. I grew so much once I started reading about the ideas and lives of different people, especially the writing of Black thinkers and activists that I never heard of in school. They were the door to my mental liberation, and I wanted others to take that journey, too.

As I re-read all these letters that I sent and received, I was processing and transforming even more. I used all that writing as a tool for my change. This kind of self-study, combined with the study of so many others' writings, made me think I had something to say. The idea to write this book really came *from* prison, from the people who surrounded me. Inside, I would share ideas and pieces of my writing with the other men, and they would show this foundational understanding of where I was coming from. My family was even encouraging, despite really having no idea what I would end up producing and just how changed I already was. They just thought it would be a positive way for me to spend time in prison, something cool for me to do. But, within the inmate community, a small group of us writers grew. It became a space for us to share our work, just like writers on the outside do. And I became a kind of go-to for providing feedback and supporting my fellow writers in processing their personal stories.

This writing group I'm talking about was not just some men sitting around with journals or writing poems and songs once in a while. We actually had many professional writers inside – some are still incarcerated today. I mention several of these authors in this book. Two writers I worked especially close with during my time in prison were Anthony Fields and Kenneth Hoffman. Fields is currently serving time in a federal penitentiary in Victorville, California. He is signed to Wahida Clark Presents Publishing and has published many of what they call "urban novels." The books are often based on his experiences as a prisoner. My other fellow writer, Kenneth Hoffman, I met while serving time at Big Sandy. He has published at least one book and multiple essays on websites that feature "carceral writing". There are so many other authors I could name who I didn't personally know – from Malcolm X to George Jackson. I am really just carrying on a tradition of writers whose work has benefited from a lot of unplanned time alone, during which we all discovered we had a lot to say.

Legacies

April 2, 2012

Marquetta,

Within the integral of respect, I greet you.

Your letters were well received. You have consistently demonstrated the acts of honor and respect with the protrusion of these correspondences. Truly, I remain impatient of your intellectual return upon my life.

I am spiritually fulfilled in knowing that you have been keeping to the obligations you once intended relative to children of special needs and to the youth at the church. It is with great comprehension for one to realize that these sorts of commitments exceed the confinements of the household, but are extensions of a nature of universality.

Concerning the information that I received from your letters that I will soon be a newly engendered grandfather, I am, perhaps, both elated and apprehensive. Elated at the behest of our royal bloodline becoming enhanced and potentially cultivated as a bloodline is considered the most sacred of all evolutionary substances. Apprehensive, though, because there may not be great sacrifices made by the collectiveness of our family that will be necessary to teach the newborn the essentials of loving via caring expressions or in how to bridge the gap that causes pain, suffering, selfdenial, dependency, and separation through the experience of a broken home. This thought upon me is fearful to the extreme. Though my need for gratitude is persistent, the thought of historical reality cannot be ignored within myself.

As I make my departure from this letter, I remind you that family can only thrive in the form of interdependency. We must learn to love self and kin before we can learn to love, and properly connect, with others that are outside of this realm. We have to cease in being satisfied with simply multiplying, but be satisfied in making great sacrifices

```
to properly evolve the family into the next
generations. I love you. And, declare my
allegiance unto this process.

                              Please be well,
                              Maurice
```

The theme of family – immediate and extended – was clearly in my mind here. I was commending my sister for the work and support she provided people not necessarily related to her. Marquetta was involved with her church community, Mt. Sinai Baptist Church, especially with the youth. My grandmother's legacy shows up in all of us once and a while, I guess. But I was also having ongoing concerns at this time about my daughter's new baby. I was afraid my daughter was not receiving all the support and care from my family necessary to continue breaking the destructive cycles of our past.

This was one more time where I was feeling helpless, trying to be a father from inside of prison. I was realizing how differently my sisters and I were seeing things lately and I worried about what they might decide to teach this latest member of the family, my grandchild. After all, as a child who had not received much love and care, I felt like I initially passed this disdain down to my own children. But now I was making changes, changing the way I even saw my own children, and I wanted that positive pattern to continue with my grandchildren. And while I was grateful that there was family support out there, I was also wary of what exactly that support was looking like – whether real and pure love was involved.

December 30, 2012

Marquetta,

Greetings Sensei. May the mastery of your wise mind lend itself to the contemplations binded into the thoughts of a brother.

Lately I've been meditating on the word love and its' usages amongst mankind. Do you believe that love could be the force that lies behind all that is good as well as all that is bad? Yes, even the bad, with its' precise and strong penetrable forces that seem to be implemented only at the individual's perception of defending something that he or she loves.

Applying this word in the context of good things is obviously hackneyed. Though, its' usage appears to be a loose fit and so vain that the energy behind its' application has a futile impact. And, its' principle seems to vary, significantly, from one person or situation to another. Meaning, if you are simply a loving person, your very first thought concerning any other person or situation should be in harmony with your personality. One's principles within their personality should never waver. I don't know, my dear sister, I'm just trying to figure out what is still real in this world.

Let's look at the bad, for instance. It is always accompanied by a strong mental passion, charged to an universal target, while being waged with unlimited enforcement upon these targets.

If it is that love is actually a real thing, then why shall its' assertion be forwarded with so many restraints when it stands before good? However, when it is aimed in the direction of bad, ie; dislike, hate, victimization, etc,. there is an exactness which must be known to all involved. When time permits, make your mind available unto me concerning this subject matter about the use of the word love by the masses.

I will now make an attempt to address the reference that you volunteered concerning your estranged husband. In light of my own personal experiences and observations, concerning the relationships between men and women in the manner of courtship or marriage, understand that each do not, by designed order, come with a guarantee of remaining solidified. This is simply because the true designed order only guarantees that people and situations will surely change, thereby, leaving some relationships to succeed and some to fail. I definitely wanted nothing but the best for the both of you in unison, but, your intimate responsibilities were not made for my involvement. My disappointment with him lies within the covenant made by any man unto his obligations to life. My duties unto these obligations likewise entail that I personally charge him with spiritual, character and dishonorable misconduct, and misrepresentation of man on the basis of selfishness, and fraudulent manliness. His willingness to fornicate with others exceeded and went far beyond the action of sexual intercourse which was dictated by a discrepancy in thought and integrity. He is first and foremost, a betrayer of himself which does not allow him to implement any value onto anything else that presents itself before him or his life. I humbly know of this man because I was this man and I should have been given, as I must give to him, the sternness of men who stood for absolute righteousness and manhood.

I must challenge you to send me some photos of the family and yourself, at your convenience. I love you... please be well.

Supreme Regards,
Brother

Love was on my mind in this letter to my sister. I was wondering to her if love could ever be "bad". Like I said, I was "trying to figure out what is still real in this world". Going through the life I had gone through, it really motivated me to question reality. And that got me wondering if love was real, and exactly what love was anyway. The way I was raised, love had a funny way of showing itself sometimes. Then I got to prison and the word *love* got used in all sorts of confusing manners.

In my essay on the mental health challenges of incarceration, which appears at the end of this book, there is some discussion regarding research around this issue. I'll just say for now that there is not much love, or intimacy, or kind human touch inside a prison. This can get a person wondering about love, looking at it from a whole new perspective, wondering if we need it and why. I was trying to understand the world in a new way, and I was looking to those people who were closest to me (family) to help me process my thoughts. This brought me to address my sister's relationship, one that theoretically should have been built on love but which seemed not to be at all.

I was a realist at this point, and I think I always had been in a way. I wanted to remind my sister that, really, nothing stays the same but change. So I was not surprised that the relationship she was in had not lasted. But, at the same time, I was thinking about the responsibilities that I believe every man should carry. The man in question had stepped out on Marquetta and, the way I saw it, her unwillingness to let him go was self-betrayal. I knew what I was talking about because I had been that man once. I only wished someone would have stepped up and challenged my behaviors back then. That's why I was pointing these things out to Marquetta.

Just like when I was writing to my sister Wanda about her relationship issues, it was easy for me to recognize what was going on because I used to play the same games these men were playing. I hold authority on these matters and felt compelled to share my knowledge with my sisters. After all, I believe we are on this earth to have experiences, to learn from them, and then to teach others our lessons.

July 25, 2013

Mother and Sister*,

I guess being physically detached from society has its' wears and tears, both on the mind and the body, but, I've learned to adapt both to every kind of terrain that befalls me. That which presents itself as the best of challenges is having my voice shut off from the minds of man's most precious species… his women.

I understand that our individual and our conjoined pasts, have demonstrated, especially in these days and times, that this kind of love spirit has been far too weakened to find solace in what I assert here, before you. It is, however, that the core of my particular understanding reflects otherwise.

I am in need of knowing from the both of you, the thought process concerning this thing. This thing being; what are your true aspirations and aims in reference to familyhood. I wrestle daily with figuring out this unknown. It is simply my desire to love you both equally and unconditionally, with respect to both your womanly nature and unique character. It seems to me that you feel challenged the very moment that I enter the space which invades the actual line of our interaction. For the sake of clarity, I must always, in a just manner, challenge you as a proponent of such family concordance. I know the essence of both of you as women and only seek to incorporate myself within its' practicality.

I make refernece that we all have experienced a long life of pain and suffering beyond our respective due process. I contend

here that it must now come to an end, especially if it was bestowed through the means of self infliction.

Would you both agree that it is past due that we extract something really great from our worldly affairs? The persecutions that are applied upon one another, within the internal portion

of our family, and the excessive self wrongs must be anniliated immediately. The evolution of great sacrificial love and honor, an element of survival for a family structure, must be perpetuated.

```
I appreciate both of you for your mental
individuality. Sis, please share the DVD
experience of mine with the rest of the
family. I divulge my loyalty and commitment
to the betterment of our nucleus.

Forever,
Maurice

* Email from author to his mother and eldest
sister.
```

During one Christmas, the United States Penitentiary, Big Sandy, allowed inmates to participate in a video program. We were given a few minutes to record a video for family or friends. I used my time to express some words of encouragement and endearment to my children. The recipient of the video was required to be on our prison visitation list, so I sent it to Marquetta. In the above letter I expressed my concern that she might have kept that video to herself, and not shown it to my kids and the family like I asked. I really wanted people to know what I was thinking, to start understanding who I had become, and I felt like she did not always support that desire.

True religion

```
October 5, 2013

Mother,

Salutation, my Honorable Matriarch… may this
letter find you in the best of spiritual,
mental, and physical health.
```

Today I took the advice from your recent correspondence and considered reflecting exclusively in the pleasure of self-indulgence, tending strickly to the contemplations of my very own heart. Afterwards, I went outside to retrieve some fresh air.

As I sat in the prison's recreation yard, I enjoyed my senses being seduced by a small quantity of nature's authority that was commanding my thoughts. I became transfixed on my worldly position within the context of multi-culturalism. It dawned on me that the other prisoners, as well as myself, are geographically separated by our devotion to our own individual dogma.

I've been respectively counseled by many of them throughout the years and they have suggested that I begin to remove myself from the practicalities of my very own acquired maxims and to instead, apply the ways of their proclaimed truisms. However, I intend to remain devoted to the practicality of self-aggrandizement and its' relation to true realism.

My Christian brothers cannot relate as to why I have not accepted Jesus Christ as my Lord and Savior. My Muslim brothers have labeled my existence as being apostate. This label is placed upon one whom disconnects himself from the initial pledge (called shahada) to Allah and the sunnah of the prophet Muhammad Ibn Abdullah. My brothers in my domicile are perplexed and suspiciously steadfast in their accusations. They are wondering why I am no longer interested in the delusions of our inherited injurious street ideals.

I've sat, in council, with the Christian community and genuinely articulated sound facts concerning my true God-self. Within these factual findings I find myself obliged to never again accept any divine teaching that bears fruit which excludes my humanistic and genetically divine rights within the whole of creation.

I have peacefully dialogued, in the company of the Islamic community, about the corrections made concerning my understanding the essence of Islam's universality. My heart yearns for the maintenance of true universal Islam, and the stabilization it brings. However, be that as it may, I was not created to live in subordination to any culture. Therefore a culture cannot be my creative decree. Through my inheritance of one culture should be placed in its' proper perspective, the following of it with another, in substitution, will inevitably render as absolutely unobtainable the knowledge of myself.

And I have, with an appropriate measure of empathy, accurately expounded to my domicile counterpart that, the victimization of us by our family and community must be healed in the core of our souls. No more entertaining our part in erroneous customs (street ideals), nor should we ignore the reasons why we were bred to uphold them.

This is something that you should have warned me about. That is, the enormous force of these authorities. My life's journey has been filled with excessiveness and eminent dangers. I've trekked through life in the worn shoes of unhappiness trying to find the meaning of my existence through ways that are not fashionably complimentary to my well being. The subordination to others on the basis of improper understanding has run its' course on this journey. Something else has readily begun, my dear mother. My knowledge of self has been empowered by these remarkable experiences and I've envisioned something that is much greater

```
in force, as well as being practical in an
originated order.

I love you and fare you well in kindness...

                                    Sincerely,
                                    SON
```

Religion, culture, and how the two relate in people's minds is interesting to me. I was telling my mom in this letter that she should have warned me just how powerful religious institutions and their ideologies are. The fact is many of us are unaware of how strong a pull religion has on us. Just think about the people who claim to kill in the name of their God. I definitely "trekked through life in the worn shoes of unhappiness" in search of a religious or spiritual identity. I had accepted basic Christianity when I was younger – enough that I could even take comfort in the readings of scripture with a fellow inmate in the hole. But for me, the consistent subordination that went along with religion became unacceptable. My experience as an imprisoned human had changed my perspective.

See, I grew up knowing I was Baptist but not really knowing much about Christianity. I was not a part of that stereotypical Black Baptist family that went to church multiple times a week and twice on Sunday. In fact, my grandmother did not attend regularly on Sundays, and I cannot even recall seeing a Bible around the house. I do remember one conversation with my grandmother, though, when she wanted to get me a suit for some church event. Having the sort of cocky attitude a twelve-year-old boy does I said, "How do you know I want to go to church, be a Christian? What if I want to be Muslim?" My grandmother gave me a look that told me that was not happening under her watch.

Co-author's note

At that young age, Islam was not something Maurice was especially familiar with, although he does recall Muslims visiting the housing projects in his old neighborhood. Beginning around the 1980s, the Nation of Islam became intent on removing the scourge of drugs from the Black community, while also creating another Black business venture, this time in the security industry. The Muslim men Maurice remembers from around his community were probably not just visiting:

> The Nation's first security experiment began in the District in 1988. When Mayfair Mansions [located in Washington DC] sought help for rampant drug dealing in the public housing complex, about 25 volunteers from Muhammad's Mosque #4 began patrolling it. The guards called themselves the Fruit of Islam -- the Nation's name for male members. By the time Farrakhan visited Mayfair Mansions in November 1988, the guards had been christened the "Dopebusters" for their success cleaning up drugs and violence. The company incorporated soon after Farrakhan's visit, hiring almost entirely Nation of Islam believers.[1]

The intentions of the organization were welcomed by many in the neighborhood for the peaceful influence their presence seemed to have had on the community. However, the fact that these security details included the sharing of the Muslim faith with fellow Black Americans had some residents complaining of proselytizing. Issues continued around these security companies, culminating in questions surrounding their financial dealings and hiring practices. This is to say that for some amount of time, in the late 1980s and early 1990s, many young African Americans were exposed – directly or indirectly – to some form of Islam. Maurice was one of them.

Many years after talking back to my grandmother, I converted to Islam. It was my first year in prison, and a friend I knew from the streets was inside with me. I had grown up with this man, we had gone to school together. I always knew him as a chaotic kind of guy, but he had changed. He was so calm, and I thought I could use some of that calmness. So, after some reflection, I took the Shahada – the testimony of Muslim faith proclaiming there is no God but Allah, and that Muhammad is the messenger of Allah. I was a Muslim.

Throughout my 20 years in prison, I often pondered religion – mine and all the others. I think because I came to Islam – to religious thinking really – as an adult, a lot of questions arose for me. That does not always happen when religion is given to you at birth. I went through a metamorphosis, starting to see connections between Islam and other spiritualities. Christianity became a much bigger idea to me than how I thought about it growing up. I was making sense of things outside of the box and speaking in ways that did not always follow the tenets of Islam – or any other major religion for that matter. Some of my Muslim brothers accused me of being too 'open'. There were specific ways to say things and commandments to follow, and I was becoming less willing to limit myself to those rules. I was even accused of being apostate, meaning I was renouncing my faith. This is a serious charge. In some Muslim communities being accused of apostasy – or just choosing to leave the religion – can be a death sentence. In the United States, it's not quite as harsh, but people in those situations are still shunned, threatened, or even attacked by fellow Muslims.

But I had come to a point in my life where I was not about to do or say anything that I did not fully believe. I had done enough of that in life already, going with the flow. In fact, going with the flow had gotten me to where I was right then. It was a lonely time for me, because I had contradicted the community where I first experienced real brotherhood. But it turned out that the questions I was asking myself – the ones that distanced me from that community – later inspired other men to ask questions, too. We were liberating our minds together.

I felt a little like a prophet; I was disrupting traditional ways of thinking and behaving in order to create more inclusive spiritual practices with a diverse group of people. I believe religions need to stand the test of time, that they require ongoing interpretation to evolve. This is the opposite of most religious practice. For the record, I still see Islam as my religious path, I just understand it from an evolutionary standpoint.

Dr. Martin Luther King, Jr. is an example of this evolution I'm talking about. King's religious path was not exactly like his parents. He was a philosophical militant the way I see it, encouraging the mixing of races and people in a way that the generation before had not. (King once brought a white woman home to his parents and his father let him know that was not going to fly). Consider

King's interest in Mahatma Gandhi's movement for Indian independence, an example of spiritual pursuit expanded. Gandhi was a man from a faraway place whose religion was quite different from Christianity, but Dr. King saw wisdom in Gandhi's nonviolent approach to the battle for Indian civil rights. In fact, many of the strategies of the Civil Rights Movement came directly from that Indian fight for independence. Religion can only benefit when it is open to what the world looks like in the present. That is my conclusion, after a few decades of thought on the subject.

Looking back

October 25, 2013

Marquetta,

Hello Sister... may things prove themselves to be virtueous with the wellness of your health.

Do you wonder what it would be like if Dad were still alive today? Believe it or not, on occasions, I do find the time to do so. I am also aware of those sharp stares which you are accustomed to bestowing on me every time there is any reference where Dad is mentioned. Though it is uncommon in our relationship and throughout our lengthly corresspondences, that you and I have never discussed the graphic details of that day when Dad's visit to my home saw the end of his life by an overdose of heroin.

After that experience, the stability of my mental health was in dire question. The motion of my forward thinking stagnated. The worse part, which held the greatest traumatic after effect, was in the disclosing of what had happened, to grandmom and to my father's wife. Agony reigned over my spirit as I listened to the sobs of these strong women and I simply wept in silence alongside their grievous affection.

On that April morning Dad phoned to inform us that he would be coming over. He said that he wanted to check out what, in particular, was wrong with the vehicle that I had previously asked him to come look at several weeks earlier. After hanging up the telephone I was rather pleased that he would be visiting and be able to spend some time with us in our new townhouse over by the Potomac Gardens Apartment complex. Mom, Talib, and myself had just moved into it.

I was awakened that night by a deep and slow voice... Son?, Son? he whispered through the crack of the door to a darken-ed room where Talib and myself had fallen asleep. Yeah Pop, what's up?, I answered. He stated; I like the place and I will come over another time to finish looking at the car, it's getting late. After waking up a bit, I began to sense that Dad had been there, at the house, for awhile before waking me. He then stated; I got to go son, I'm tired, I'm real tired. I replied; Pop if you're tired, chill out here until morning so you can rest. He stated; Naw Son, I don't mean physically tired, but more mentally. I am about to walk home, I'll call you later. I replied; Don't walk home, it's too far. I understand that you're not bothered by walking, but call a taxi and I'll pay for it… wake me up when it arrives. I could sense the familiar look that would come across his face every time I would offer him money (which he would always decline. He replied; All right Son, I'll call a taxi.

Some time later that night Mom woke me up with a strange anxiety in her voice… Maurice, wake up! I answered; What's up Mom? She said; Come and get your father. Where is he? He's in the hallway, laying on the floor. I got up, went into the hallway, and told him to get up. I then shook him a couple of times and when he did not respond, I turned and asked Mom what was wrong with him. She answered; When I got up to use the bathroom he was there, in that spot. I then asked her; Had he been drinking? She answered; Yeah, a little. I then told her to go grab me a blanket and pillow out of the closet so that I could make him a pallet on the floor where he was laying, in an attempt to allow him to sleep off what was left of his intoxication.

I rose the following morning believing that I would engage my father in conversation over some breakfast cooked by my mother, which was something that never had been done prior to that day. There, laying on the hallway floor, still wrapped in the make shift bed, with every blanket tuck and body limb stationed in the exact same position as I had placed them the night before, was Dad's rigormortised form. The body was illuminated by the ceiling sky roof that was fixed over the hallway floor.

It is not an understatement to write that the entire scene completely paralyzed the wits out of Mom, Talib, and myself. Right there, I needed to bring forth some much needed and requisite answers while I settled into the perplexity of the situation. I searched for these answers by examining the contents of his pockets. In the same area where I found a hunter's knife, wallet, watch, and ten dollar bill, I discovered the origins of this silent tragedy.

The plastic baggy contained the residue of a powdery substance and a used syringe with traces of blood on it. This evidence spoke very clearly as to what had happened. Our father had overdosed in the wake of visiting my home. Only through further investigation did I find out that it was my father's favorite choice of narcotics, heroin.

Unbeknown to myself, but according to the so called drug dealer, Dad had been using heroin for a long time. My complete ignorance of his symptoms haunts my soul to this very day. Maybe, if I was abreast of this fact, I could have further investigated his sudden and bizarre blackout. Instead, I relied solely on the information given to me by my mother who, also unbeknown by me, also shared in my father's habits.

Perhaps I now understand that you were allowing me as much time as I needed to express this situation to you. For that reason, I thank you and humbly admire your patience. I ask that you all forgive me my ignorance. Had I known, you know that much would have been attempted to preserve the quality of my father's life.

I love you with honors, and divulge completely, my conscious observation of the quality of your being…

Sincerely,
Brother

In this letter I was confronting the subject of our father. His death was traumatic, for many reasons. Maybe the hardest part was having to give my grandmother the news. Once again, I was using these letters to process, first writing them, and then by re-reading them. So in this one, I kind of narrate to my sister the events that led up to my father's death. I had kept them to myself for so long.

Pops was coming over for a visit, saying he was going to help me fix the car – a request I had made weeks before, by the way. I suspected that my father might also be interested in spending some alone time with his estranged wife, too – my mother. But I was looking forward to his visit. We had just recently moved into Potomac Gardens, a housing project located on G Street SE, thirteen blocks from the Capitol building. I was excited to show him around the new place I had gotten for me, my mother, and Le'mia, my daughter.

My daughter was not there that evening, but my cousin, Talib, was visiting. We smoked some weed together that night and ended up going to bed early, before my parents did. Drugs were a constant presence in my family's life, but my parents' habits were always more serious than mine. They used the hard stuff. For me, it wasn't until I was in prison, in isolation and despair, that I used heroin. I never actually witnessed my parents' drug-taking, but I always knew for a fact that they were both addicts.

As I wrote to my sister in this letter, at some point that night my father stuck his head into the room where Talib and I were sleeping. He told me he liked the apartment, and that he'd take a look at the car another time. No surprise that Pops did not actually complete the task he had supposedly come over to do in the first place. In my foggy brain I wondered to myself what he had been up to all that time because I knew he'd been there for a while. Anyway, he said he was tired and needed to get home. Growing up, 'tired' was something my father was a lot. I was used to seeing him tired, which could look like a lot of different things. Sometimes he was so tired I couldn't even wake him up from his sleep. I definitely did not want him walking home in a compromised state that night.

I was still half asleep and probably still high, but I suggested to my father that he either stay the night at the apartment or call a taxi and I would pay for it. He said he would call the taxi and wake me back up when it arrived. Apparently, that taxi never got called. A while later I was woken up again, this time by my mother. I knew something was wrong by the sound of her voice. "Come and get your father," she said. I made my way to Pops, lying in the hallway, and began the familiar task of attempting to wake him. When he did not awake no one was especially concerned; it was not the first time they had seen him out cold. My mom acted like nothing out of the ordinary had been going on when I asked. So I got some blankets and a pillow and covered him up where he was. The expectation being that, once again, he would get up when he was ready.

The next morning I woke up, looking forward to a rare moment of family time; both of my parents there in the same place, all of us actually having breakfast together. Instead, I came upon my father lying in the exact same place as I had left him the night before. It was clear that he was dead. My response was to literally start searching for answers. And I found them in his pocket: a plastic bag of white powder and a used syringe. Heroin had always been the drug of choice for my parents and in the end it took them both, in different ways.

In this letter to my sister, I am trying to express the frustration and anger I felt surrounding this event. For one thing, I felt partly responsible. I mean how could a man like me, who dealt in drugs myself, be so ignorant about what had been happening? Yet I was also frustrated with my mother, who had not been honest earlier that night when I had asked about my father's situation.

After my father's death, I finally began to look into his habit, like what he took and who sold it to him. But in a way it felt ignorant, and hypocritical, of me to pursue this line of questioning. Did I not deal in these same drugs myself? Did I not believe that the responsibility was on the user not the seller? Even my mother agreed. "Your father has a habit of over-injecting" she told me. So that was that.

I was sick

January 30, 2014

Marquetta,

Hello Sister...

Today is the first opportunity I've been given to correspond with the outside world since my surgery* 10 days ago. The brewing of my temper has my blood pressure up and my sternum is killing me each time that I cough, which happens everytime that I try and speak. For reasons that are totally unclear to me, I have been locked in an isolation cell designed for prisoners assigned to suicide watch. I have been in this room for the past two days, 24 hours per day. I am without the medications that were prescribed by the hospital and I have been offered nothing but fried foods and other fare that is high in sodium and fats.

The officials are walking pass pretending that I am not even here. Up to this very moment, I haven't even had so much as my blood pressure checked. Though my mind has begun to slip, because of this blatant abuse, into a state of depression, what I find strange is, however, that I appreciate the administration's version of psycho-logical and and physical malpractice. This is because typically a prisoner would place an overly unwarranted trust in the administration to do the right thing in protecting the psychological and physical health of the inmate. But here, with me, their inability and disregard to rehabilitate a prisoner is clearly demonstrated. This disregard goes beyond the physical recovery from a medical procedure and is a further indication of their failure to protect main society by preparing prisoners for integration back into that society. Instead, the prisoner, through every turn of their imprisonment, is subject to the full expression of all the elements of inhumaneness.

My dear sister, why I have been subjected to this treatment of punishment, simply because I have become ill, is beyond my understanding. It also makes absolutely no sense that I have to send you this correspondence through a third party source. I have not been afforded the right to correspond with my family for any reason, let alone after experiencing such a traumatic medical procedure. You must, with great impetus, contact the appropriate authorities so they will immediately review this matter in order that I may receive the proper recovery treatment. This will,

```
perhaps, prolong my life or, at worst, at
least save it from imminent danger.

                                    Sincerely,
                                      Brother

*The author underwent triple by-pass open
heart surgery
```

I was pretty sick by the end of 2013. Once I was finally diagnosed with heart disease, I underwent triple bypass surgery. The post-operative unit at Hazleton Penitentiary – where I had been sent specifically because of my heart condition – turned out not to be the best place to heal. There was a sort of ironic truth in the situation: the lack of attention and care I got from prison staff there – even for an inmate who had undergone major surgery that came with all sorts of risks – illustrated how little the penal system cared about the prison population. Like, the people in charge wouldn't even attend to the basic needs of a post-operative patient, so they certainly weren't going out of their way to help rehabilitate people (the alleged mission of our prison system).

Inhumanity was everywhere during my time in prison. In this instance I felt like I was being punished for getting sick. But why? Did the extra labor required to take care of a sick inmate seem like too much? I guess I was "just a convict" to most of them. And then, all of a sudden, my communications were restricted – and next they put me on suicide watch. In this letter I make it clear that this was truly a stressful experience, like I really felt out of control – even more than usual. And alone, isolated in that dangerous way I had been trying to keep away from all those years. I asked Marquetta to alert the authorities as soon as possible to the fact that something very wrong was happening to me. I might have been placed on suicide watch, but I really wanted to live.

A kind of freedom

March 29, 2014

Mother,

Greetings at the behest of respect. May it suffice that I write I love you, as this shall be the required duty of a son upon his mother.

Despite what you wrote in your latest correspondence, invoking the word "mother," while needing to apply sonship to its meaning, has always been reserved in my heart for you. By your own intent, you have chosen not to receive what is right-fully yours. You would not have entertained these thoughts if only you could have been there to witness the pain in me since your absence.

Before I continue, you must be given the reason that I say/write the things that I do, and the reasons for such. First, and foremost, it has absolutely nothing to do with my placement of blame, being bitter from my illness, or asking of you for answers that are irrational. You seem to think very lowly of me, Mother. Once again, you are attempting to divert my basic request for information, at the unjust gesture of self-pity, and manipulation. Fortunately, your tactics have been met with the sterness of request's purity. My requests are very clear, and fair, absent of any hint of malice behind them. This your heart is soundly aware of.

Our current physical illness should never be used as shields to reject our duties to one another. If for no other reason, when we are hurting, there are others who are hurting as well, in spite of what our minds may be suggesting. Honor is due in this respect, while nothing which is in the nature of selfishness shall prevail. Our experiences, at the behest of love, should be shared in appropriate measures to bring the dignified closure which our strained spirits have been yearning for, for so many years. And, we will always be in a state of lonliness as long as we continue to isolate our respective life's journey from the same people who share in the process of our evolutionary duties.

I am now obliged to place an insert from your correspondence dated March 27, 2014, in its proper perspective. It read, "Maurice, when you had your freedom you really didn't give a damn about me. But still, I didn't and don't blame you for anything..."

First, my beloved mother, I have never been afforded an opportunity to feel real freedom. Since my conception I have ceaselessly been chained to something, or to someone, which left me restricted, while, from the beginning, lacking the mental, physical, and spiritual protection of yourself......Yet, and still, I didn't and don't blame you either.

The primary dictator of our relations lies solely in the heart of yourself. From the very inception, it has always, in an unprecedented manner, been about you. It was your undisciplined behavior, and logic that led your abandonment of me. It was these things of yours that ushered me to live with my grandmother. you never visited throughout the years, at least in an attempt to restore all which you had sacrificed of our mother and son connection. And so, it was your lack in giving a damn that mortalized my ability to understand how to give a damn. Mother, you must be compelled to know that, for every misfortune that you've suffered under, its cause affected the very core of the vulnerable children you conceived. It is not my aim to revisit these past misconducts; they only resurface at the call of your own wrong inferences, not mine. My aim is, and always has been in the context of clarity, reconciliation, love, and the strengthening of our relations for the benefit of ourselves, and future generations, period. The facts are, we have lived our lives in a coarse manner, based on the cards we were dealt. But, it is no longer about you and I; those accusation to which you, yourself are being subjected, are then faced by your children, and I, myself will also be subjected to stand by the curiosity, and unfulfilled hearts of my children. Just as I have approached you, I must also make preparations, for I too will have to face my rightful accusers in a state of humbleness, and honor for the connection of father and children.

Thank you, for the funds for which I have immense gratitude. Tell the hubby to keep his head up throughout his struggle, though things will only get better at the force of his will, so project his best. Be mindful that my admiration of you will undyingly stand intact always. I charge you with one displeasing act, however. It is not that you do not know me as you should, but, it is the fact that you do not try your best

```
in attempting to do so, and this concerns
me greatly.
                            I REGARD YOU SUPREME,
                                                Son
```

I had grown deeply philosophical in prison, thanks to a lot of time spent reading, writing, and thinking. My approaches to life, and love, and my illness, reflected this outlook. The word *philosophy* literally means 'love of wisdom', and I was spending more and more time on my quest for that wisdom.

In this letter to my mother, I was wrestling with her unwillingness to communicate directly with me. I was done with all that stuff I grew up with: the defensiveness, the pity, the anger. We were taught to keep things to ourselves, but I wanted answers to the questions formulating inside of me. Unfortunately, human beings often depend on defense mechanisms when they get caught up in these kinds of conversations. Sometimes we don't even know we're defending ourselves because it's become second nature. Therapists say that these kinds of tools were probably necessary at some point in our lives and that's why we have them. But the wisdom is in knowing when not to use them anymore.

I had been preparing myself to connect more closely with other human beings – it was the only way I was going to process life so far. But this was too much for my mother, which I see as a kind of selfish stance, as she was ignoring how her behavior affected me and her other children. She accused me of not giving "a damn" about her even when I had my "freedom". If that's what you want to call freedom. It was like she was the kid and I was the parent, like it was my duty to be an engaged human while growing up in a highly dysfunctional world – a world she helped create. In the letter she "forgives" me for this. She had a long way to go in the processing department, that's for sure.

I addressed this comment of hers in the letter, explaining that freedom was not something I experienced in my childhood. See, even though the prison system seemed fully unable to address my mental health at that point, I had been working to heal myself inside. The New Testament reads: "And be not conformed to this world: but be ye transformed by the renewing of your mind…" (Romans 12:2). For a while, I had definitely conformed to the world created by people like my parents, until I became committed to renewing my mind.

I was intentional about my transformation, about taking advantage of all those hours inside prison to process my way to better mental health. This, I understood from reading and talking to people, involved reconnecting with the disconnected. As a father, I began to see what I had already done to my children. But I also knew there was time to stop the trend, to reverse the cycle of my own upbringing. I was working out relations with my family so that I could give family to my own children, just the way my grandmother wanted it to be.

I ended this letter appealing to my mother to try to get to know me, the man I was becoming. Prison is not a place where we are seen as individuals, as people with stories or loves or ideas. But, at least, if I could get my family to see me – *not* as the same man who was convicted of murder at age 27, but a very different man who was working hard to reform himself while surrounded by chaotic prison life – then that would be one step forward.

Unfortunately, my family has had a very difficult time making this adjustment, even once they were able to see me face to face.

```
April 20, 2014
```

Marquetta,

It is my honor to make known my regard, supreme regard, as I uphold your status as Matriarch, and your well-being..

Here lately, you have been giving me the appearance

of a very busy person. I can relate perfectly if this appearance is a factual look, and dearly am apologetic if I'm being a bit selfish by observing this in a aspect of avoidance, self-confinement, or deliberate incommunicado. Hopefully, I am completely off base, and that my perception has a major descrepancy in its conclusion. However, please make your state of mind known, as sincere communication, in spite of its contents, is the basis of what you, and I are use to inheiring too.

The traumatic time spent in that hospital bed gave me plenty of opportunity to ponder on my current position in life. It has informed me that too much valueable time is being wasted. It informed me that, if I had died in the course of the operation, so much would have gone unfinished, and unencroached. Though self-preservation shall be the first obligation of a person, the liberation of my body from prison, and the solidarity of our family unit is the top priority on my list of things which must be completed, or in intense progress before I make a departure from this physical earth.

Deviation can never be considered for me. Because for me, it is a matter of life, or death. It is a matter of eternal life, or death for the spirit in the bliss and culture decreed within the provision of family matters. And, for an equitable duty to the spirit of the legacy, which is imperative upon all mankind.

This family unification thing, we must get right. Pure fundamentals. The basis, which entails that we are not to be overwhelmed by personal ideologies, others, or the defects within ourselves. Our goal should simply coincide with what is our true humanity. We shall be grounded in this by our discipline and love, and allow all whom choose to convene in our space, the luxury of witnessing a natural expedition.

If my dear sister, this is not to be, it would be for me like dying twice. First, a very long and vain spiritual and mental death before the necessary physical one. Please, work diligently at preventing this from occurring for us.

Send my regards to the family….

I command your wellness,
Brother

This letter to my sister echoes what I wrote to my mother. But with my sister I could be a little more straight in explaining my desire to connect the family. How can I explain that when we humans are put to a physical test – one that comes with possibilities of death – our priorities change? Family connection was already a motivating factor for me in that prison, but my illness made things feel more urgent. I needed my family to know and share in this understanding, and I was so frustrated by their blindness to the crisis that was surrounding us.

Tell somebody

August 16, 2014

Marquetta,

Homage Kindred Spirit….may all fare itself well in your endeavors.

My dear sister, the purpose of this letter is to inform you of my current circumstances here at the institution.

I have been learning on a daily basis that, this institution is atrocious, and that is from the top of the food chain, to its bottom. Corruptive practices plagues every movement of these administrators. Thievery, lying, medical murder, etc. There is no way that I can remain here in the midst of this decorated wickedness.

This is not a message of help, but one which makes you aware of the events that may subsequently happen in the near future if these things continue to afflict me.

At this very moment, the prison is on lockdown, and may be as such for awhile. Though, not on account of the particular medications that I am taking, my health may not withstand a lot of these high sugared, sodium, and processed foods, and lack of exercise. This is what I told you was, justifiable medical murder. Under any circumstances, please do not allow their dishonesty to prevail. If I am incommunicado in the days ahead, you now understand its reason, and what it is that must be done.

I have not been to a followup exam with a cardiologist since the operation. What reasonable health care provider allows a patient no opportunity to be reevaluated after such an operation and complications?

I will enclose the information to the attorney that

```
I spoke with here at the institution recently
about these issues. Contact her in regards to
myself in the event you do not hear from me.
Perhaps I'll see you shortly….
                              Please be well,
                              Brother
```

When I re-read these letters, I see how my tone got more and more urgent. I did try to describe a little of what was happening around me at Hazelton, but there was no way they could have handled everything I saw. The United States Penitentiary Hazelton, in West Virginia, is not a nice place to be.

As I say in the letter to my sister, I was *not* receiving the medical care needed for my heart condition. And, once again, I asked my sister to reach out to someone in charge, to let somebody know what was happening at that place. I don't know if she ever did but, realistically, I also know that it takes more than a few complaints from some private citizens to change the American prison system.

Co-author's note

Maurice's characterization of Hazelton as "not a nice place" is an understatement. The penitentiary is "one of the prisons that generates the most outspoken protest", according to research done by the organization *More Than Our Crimes (MTOC)*. In September of 2022, *MTOC* solicited stories from inmates about their various carceral institutions. Even as sharing these stories is in itself "an act of bravery when officers are known for retaliation", tales abounded regarding Hazelton.

From banishment to the "hole" or SHU (Special Housing Unit) for filing a grievance against prison staff, to being refused hospital care as a patient confined to a wheelchair with leg infections, to disregarded COVID protocols, it was clear there was a highly dysfunctional environment at play in Hazelton.[2] Additionally, a 2018 article from the Associated Press reported:

> In February 2015, an inmate stabbed a fellow [Hazelton] prisoner with a hand-crafted weapon during a fight, according to court documents. Another inmate received an extended sentence in May for assaulting a fellow prisoner and possessing a deadly weapon. "There are a multitude of federal prisons that don't have a homicide rate like that," said Cameron Lindsay, a former federal prison warden who now works as a jail security consultant.[3]

Lest we think there have been improvements, on October 11, 2023, *MTOC* posted on Instagram that the Justice Department had set up an internet hotline for prisoners to report abuses at the Hazelton complex. Turns out that prison officials were caught blocking the email address that accessed the hotline.

October 16, 2014

Mother,

Greetings my beloved Matriarch...

You know Mom, when a typical Blackman that is raised in the ghettos start to reflect on his death on this earth, it is usually by the infliction of some sort of malicious force, particularly to the outer body. This death is thought about bitterly, but in great anticipation of its inevitable circumstances. However, when the gander of its reality begins to show up through his inner being, via the miscarriage of his thought processes, and the circumstantial forecast is no longer the cast because it has been overshadowed by an undignified possibility of inefficiency. Mom, for the Blackman who tries desperately to use every inch of his brain forces to maintain survival, which is the majority, this is upon himself the utter experience of torture.

My thought are being strained here daily by the instability of my mind, which is making concentration very exhausting. I do admit of being frightened by the fact of my mental organ's failure, and that I am spending more time learning how to maintain its stability than using its propelling resources to make progress in my current situation.

The depression disorder which our family has been sharing since long as I can remember, has become steadfast in frequency. And, the fullness of paranoia distracts the protrusion of my rationale almost at the very same pace.

I've been studying more of myself here in the last few years. The engima of the mind's flow is interesting, and if it is all possible, should only be tampered with, by its owner, especially in the cause of evolution. I suggest evolution being that he will evolve perfectly with his defectiveness, regardless of his unwillingness, or willingness to want to do so. The details of survival depends upon it.

Though the most peculiar part of this is that, loneliness plays an intricate role, however, I should. On account that the average individual, or system is too rudiment of themselves, and would have to have undergone an intense study of themselves, while also admiring the elements of their very own defects to even begin to relate to this issue. Observe my circumstances here in prison. Imprisonment has surely assisted significantly in inflaming this imbalance, but cannot in no way assist in its leveling. I must rely on myself to identify, and repair myself.

I will close out now my beloved Matriarch…. Please, find the motivation in each day to motivate someone in the cause of peace, and please be well.

Son

In this letter you can really hear my desperation. It's hard for me to read it. I am explaining more plainly the ways my mind was feeling tortured, and how depression (a family trait) had landed in me. I was starting to get real tired of the battle against all the outside influences attacking my mind and spirit. Evolution was becoming exhausting, and I was clearly seeing my situation as related to my being a Black man. That's what I was pointing out in the letter, that there was something especially painful for me and my brothers, being kept away from our own thoughts and feelings there. I felt like I was speaking for a lot of us in that letter.

I think this was ancestral memory working inside of me. My body was remembering the centuries of brainwashing by those in power. Part of slavery's strategy was to isolate people to control them. This seemed intentional at the prison too, and that loneliness attacked our mental health. So, I reached out to the people who I could by writing letters. I shared my thoughts so I could link myself with another person. I wanted my family to continue that process with me – and with each other – because I have seen what it looks like when people give up on humanity, when they isolate, or are forcefully isolated. Those people die alone. I did not want to walk this path and I wanted to warn people when I saw them walking that path. People didn't always listen though.

3
Sankofa

September 20, 2010

Le'mia*,

May this epistle be received by my intriguing princess with the warmest attributes of a father's love and admiration for such human royalty.

It has come to my attention, via our latest telephone conversation, that you are not always authentic with me in the issues that you assert. Again, I must remind you of the extraordinary bond that we are supposed to be upholding that is not, in any sense, about judgment or foul criticism concerning any matter. I hold in my possession the highest degree of honor, respect, and a divine inclination towards you that is commanded by ancestral inheritances. Nothing or no one shall disturb this sacred bond.

Throughout the life of our correspondences, there will be numerous differences concerning the individuality in views, ideologies, perspectives, and applications. With this understanding we will gain the knowledge and respect for both the uniqueness of the individual and the diversity in the outlooks of others. My personal theory is that this may be, in part, the remedy that will medicate our dysfunctional attempt at integration into our family's sick infrastructure.

That is the rationale which we must prepare to communicate on. The honorable one that strengthens the health of our family and ourselves. Truth renders itself as extremely important and results in doing away with faulty communication which is something we must do. The lack of truth has absolutely no place in relations that are bound together by the threads of natural purity. You are the Creator's purest of gifts that are deployed within the intimacy of my life. And, I will sacrifice this same life to protect what is a phenomenal gift.

I love you infinitely and I love you daily. And, in this sense, let us build upon a communal that reflects or uncontaminated bond.

Love,
Father

* Author's eldest daughter

It became important to me to erase the patterns of my upbringing and, instead, make new ones with my kids. I was in prison, but I was still a father and I wanted to make sure my children understood that honesty was the only way we were going to grow – both as a family and as individuals. Le'mia is my oldest, born in 1989, so I felt she would understand this best. Le'mia believes God speaks to her through me, something like that. We were the closest, too, because I had been able to be her father on the outside the longest. Understand, I was around for all my kids at some point, and they all knew each other – even though they had different mothers. That was just what family looked like at that point.

I am generally very proud of Le'mia. She graduated high school with honors, then went to Prairie View A&M University in Texas, a Historically Black College and University (HBCU). She studied Special Education there and is a schoolteacher now. She has three children. When I told her about the book that I wrote, the letters and commentary I put together, she was inspired to write a book, too. She wrote about her college years. I edited that book for her. It was a great way to connect. I really hope she gets it published at some point.

Instincts

November 13, 2010

Imani*,

Greetings at the behest of respect. May it suffice to write that I love you, as this should be the duty of a father upon his daughter.

I received your latest correspondence today. I will send you more mailing stamps so that you will not have to hold your thoughts and letters that you write to me any longer than is required.

I need to speak to you and your mother where it concerns your living arrangements as soon as you can get together. What is the current status of that arrangement?

It is important, in the extreme, that you and I discuss, in depth, this multiple array of boyfriends thing that you have going on. It is normal and healthy for you to be engaged in appropriate social relations with the opposite gender. However, you must and by all means be safe and certain of these relations. You suggested to me that you felt strange concerning this one particular young man. I reminded you in the past that if you are feeling strange about a young man or anything, you must pay very close attention to those feelings. They are the feelings that I told you about concerning your womanly intuition. It is your inner ears listening to something that is conveying a message to you. Remember, "You can hear even through no one is making a sound".

Slow down princess and enjoy the company of someone by getting to know their character and by understanding their nature. Write back soon.

                        I Command Your Happiness,
                                        DAD

* Author's youngest daughter

Here I am feeling frustrated again, trying to be a father to my youngest from far away. It was sounding to me like Imani was not valuing herself enough, just giving herself away – like my sisters were sometimes doing. I wanted to remind my daughter that she was valuable, and that her instincts were something to be listened to.

In the Muslim faith, instincts are part of the spiritual heart. In Christianity they might get called the Holy Spirit. I believe women have exceptional instincts; they just don't always follow them. I should know, because I was with some women who probably knew better than to be with me. I was with Imani's mother the longest – we all lived together and my daughter and I were very close then. She was around eight years old when I went to prison. Once I got arrested, Imani shut off all verbal communications with everyone. She would not talk, just keeping to herself for a long time. That was very hard because we had really been buddies at one time.

She still comes to me sometimes now, whether it's for advice or just to check in, but I don't think she has forgiven me for going to prison. Our relationship is off for other reasons, too, I think. I want more for her than she wants for herself. It seems that way with all my children, actually. That gets me upset. I understand Imani had it rough and probably deals with a lot of issues because of my situation. But she has so much to offer, and I don't see the motivation in her. She has her kids and doesn't take anything much else seriously. I guess people would say it's unfair for me to even have an opinion about Imani as a woman and mother, seeing as how I wasn't there to help guide her, and with all what I did. I do know motherhood in and of itself is something a man, in my opinion, cannot even fathom. So, whatever my opinions may be on these topics, it's really not my business to share them with her. I know that to be true.

Co-author's note:

Parenting from prison was addressed from a father's viewpoint in the last chapter. But what about the children? There is much research and experiential evidence on that subject, including many firsthand testimonies from those who have grown up with their parents behind bars. The research shows a clear correlation between lack of self-esteem, lack of motivation, and having a parent in prison.

A 2015 report sponsored by Child Trends – a nonprofit research organization – found that: "Having an imprisoned parent is an example of a loss that is not socially approved or (often) supported, which may compound children's grief and pain, leading to emotional difficulties and problem behaviors."[1] These experiences can, in turn, be isolating for young people such that active withdrawal by the children from all sorts of life activities, including engagement with their parents, occurs. Interestingly, this study also shows that there are many children of incarcerated parents who do *not* present with the majority of problems and difficulties used as measurements in this study. Ultimately, Imani's lack of motivation – as perceived by her father – may or may *not* be directly correlated to his incarceration.

Ancestral patterns

April 10, 2011

Le'mia,

Greetings. Let the divine affinity of womanhood and motherhood enter your life with virtue, and the understanding which is natural within this union.

That yearning you feel towards men is natural. Engaging in proper sexual intercourse because of those feelings is also natural. Becoming impregnated at the behest of this intercourse is as normal as living or dying. What renders itself as unnatural or abnormal is bringing into fruition an innocent soul without setting up to reliably provide for the well being of their soul. It's abnormal that an innocent soul should not be unconditionally loved, housed, nurtured and understood. It is said that when you procreate you must be willing to help create the mental and spiritual life that is contained in the physical being you helped to produce. You must be willing to spend the time and energy that is part of this creative process. In this I agree. I must, therefore, correct your comments concerning what you see as the adversity in this matter. The only adverse element associated with childbirth is the existence of an ill prepared parent.

Your ambition to complete school and the commitment to your (our) unborn child is mentally euphoric to me. I must project that you are an extraordinary woman who embodies the genetic codes of the warrior hearted spirit of our ancestors. This projection is ensued by the familiarity of the kinship between you and I, which has gratefully opened my heart.

Question: What do I want for my offspring?

I need you to consciously build on the "each one, teach one" formula. As we shall teach, and learn from one another, I need you to become rooted in the love of your ancestors, the people in your lineage, from whom you possess both their physical appearance and spirit. You must fulfill this obligation to show the 300 million or so of our ancestors that their great sacrifices are appreciated.

It is my humble request that my offspring learn to love by expression. Helping, complimenting, honoring, building with, caring for, educating, providing for, nurturing, respecting, admiring, and protecting each other as a family of people should and must do. In so doing, we begin to bridge the gap that caused pain, suffering, broken homes, self denial, separation, and genocide to our people during and after our ancestor's enslavement.

This request is not prejudice in nature, but, it is my viewpoint that integration has largely failed us as a people because of our failure to build from our own ethical base. This view should be looked at in the light of our tribal foundation, ie; our immediate family. We can no longer evolve thoughts and actions consisting of cultural deficiencies. it is also said that cultural awareness provides you with a philosophy, a standard, and a frame-work from which you can approach life. African culture, for example, navigates on the philosophy of "we" rather than "I" within its' oriented framework. People are not thought to be isolated and left to fend for themselves.

I conclude that I will aid and assist my grandchild, and yourself, with all my realistic capabilities. I first need you to learn and teach your siblings their African essence and responsibilities as they have been taught their American essence and responsibilities. The universality of knowing them both in their exactness will offer all of you the grounding that will be called upon in your life in all aspects of living.

My departure is met by declaring my allegiance to you,

Father

I'm saying to my daughter here what I know to be the truth. While she was concerned about her pregnancy, I was more concerned with the life of the baby after it was born. Even though I lived my life in a way that might not look like it, I always knew somewhere how important it was for a child to have a stable home. It was like, for a time, I was going against exactly what I knew just because I didn't know how to do right. And I sure didn't know how to ask for help. So, I had babies. But I cared, too. That's why I did what I did to support them. I thought I was doing right by my family. That's what I mean about "going with the flow" – it was my approach to too many things back then. I didn't want my little girl making the same mistakes.

By the time I wrote this letter to Le'mia, I had really soaked up my grandmother's viewpoint that we were all connected, that family wasn't just blood relatives alive today, but it was all those who lived before us. How else could we Black people get stronger unless we remembered to look back while we moved forward? It's like the African Sankofa bird, symbolizing going back to get it, then using that *it* to inform the future. My experience in prison brought me many things, including – maybe ironically – a renewed connection to my identity as an African American, a Black man in America. I wanted my children to experience that ancestral connection, too, and then to pass it down to their own children.

Le'mia became pregnant with her first child, Ali, a few years after this discussion. Apparently, she had ideas about having a child for quite some time, but finishing college was her priority. After she graduated, she shared with me her plans on having a child, when she visited me at FCI Butner. Who the father would be, she told me, wasn't much of a concern. She just wanted a child; abortion was never going to be an option for her. Those were her feelings, while my feelings as a father were utter terror. I didn't want her making children with just anyone for the sake of being a mother; the man she had in mind at the time was not at all what she had once said she wanted. But in the end my position was to support whatever direction she chose to go in.

She married the man in question, and then had two more children with him. He is not involved with his children anymore, but this comes as no surprise. Le'mia had wanted to change him into someone he never signed up to be. And that was my biggest concern all along; her trying to force the issue. In the end she would not get what she wanted, and the kids would have to suffer through their parents' terrible marriage. This is what happens when you pile roses on top of crap. It's still crap when you get down to it, and no amount of ceremony or childbearing will change that.

February 9, 2012

Le'mia,

In light of all my created astonishings, I submit here that you are the most intriguing of its' magnificent granduer.

Upon these attempts at the rebuilding of our meaningful relationship, there must be a disclosure of information that is prevelant to your conclusive thoughts of me.

Before I came to live with my paternal grandmother, which is only what you have known of me, I once lived with my mother, two elder sisters, and an elder brother. My mother was a decent working oriented woman. But, the course of things changed drastically once my mother had been overwhelmed by the elements of abusive men and substance abuses, which included alcholism. I presume, by the force of these authorities, she became extremely physical and mentally abusive towards my siblings and myself. These abuses delved into such categories as broken bones and attempted drowning. At some point my siblings grew tired of my mother's actions and dislodged themselves from our home to go and live with their friends and other family. I was left alone at the tender age of perhaps 6 or 7 to absorb the fullness of those forceful authorities, and psychotic behaviors.

It is needless to elaborate upon this set of atrocious circumstances that led to my mother and I moving from one person's house to another. I was eventually accepted into the home of my paternal grandmother with whom I lived upon your introduction into this world.

Considering both of our realities, my paternal grandmother did everything, within reason and ability, to ease my transition into a life that would be considered normal and befitting for a young child. She herself was an elderly unemployed Black woman, trying to survive on a fixed income while living in a small subsidized apartment with my uncle and cousin. This you are fully aware of.

As it has been studied, projected, and written previously, no child can suffer that type of ordeal without paying the penalty for entering this realm of acute malicious pummels. Through the body may heal, the injury to the mind and spirit will need the careful procedures of reconstructive surgery.

Since then, I have lived with a degree of these injuries both in and outside of my fatherhood. On the basis of why I was feeling and acting as I was during your upbringing, I have come to label those times as, "unidentifiable chaotic dysfunctions" reflecting absolute mental and spiritual confusion in my duties to fatherhood.

I messed up concerning your right to expect me to protect and secure your growth and development. It involves a great amount of risk to expose to you the fact that I played that role in depriving you of all its' fundamental components. Truly, I brought forth your existence, but, did not know enough to love myself enough to love you efficiently. It is even more painful and embarrassing admitting these things only after entering the threshhold of incarceration. I am, without doubt, shameful and regretful that I never offered you your value and self worth as a human being or woman. You are a priceless gem that cannot be appraised. Surely, you are my most sacred triumph. And, even though loving you is cool, I enjoy you, living through me, more. I, with sincerity, promise that the promotion of your essence will never go forgotten.

I bid your authority,
Father

Le'mia was 23-years-old when I wrote this letter and I felt it was time to share a little more of what my early life was like with her. It's not that I wanted my daughter to feel sorry for me, or that I was making excuses for my mistakes. I just wanted her to understand me, to increase our connection through honesty and clarity. She was old enough now to hear these stories, though I left out details that I felt were not necessary for her to hear.

In a lot of ways, I was telling myself these stories again, and for the first time. I mean that I was really taking the time to let the reality of what I went through sink in. It helped me make a better connection with myself, too. Looking back to move forward and all. These letters in general are part confession and part explanation. I started trying to forgive myself for all that I had done to my life and to others' lives, too.

March 27, 2012

Imani,

Greetings, my beloved princess. May this epistle find you in a state of understanding the meaning and connection to the spirit of your co-creator... your father.

Do you remember, during the beginning of my incarceration, when your grandmother brought you to the prison to see me? I was so engulfed in emotion, being that I hadn't seen you in such a long time, that I could not even speak for the first few minutes. Do you have any idea what radicalizes a father's emotions to the point of speechlessness?

Perhaps it is beyond definition. Nonetheless it is so powerful that, sometimes, I can feel that which you are feeling at certain moments, in spite of the distance that separates us.

My tears on that day signaled, in an unintentionally overt manner, that my being incarcerated will subject my little girl to the deciphering of every circumstance and emotion with only the guidance of very own immature mentality. It is that you must be afforded the opportunity to have your fragile mentality nurtured by the authority of your father's maturely guided mentality.

Yes, you have to inform your mother of your suspected impregnation.

In regards to your health, there may be another human being within you that requires, not secrecy, but, for its' health to be attended to at the behest of you. Being kicked out of the home is the least of all your worries. And, kicking you out of places yet again places another human being at risk of being in harms way. This is in spite of the circumstances that surround the both of you as your mother truly understands. These are simply wasted attempts of non-beneficial energies.

This suspected child was conceived by the act of Thomas and yourself and now you must place the entirety of your life to prevent any situation that will bring harm its' way... spiritually, mentally, or physically.

You have allowed circumstances to dictate the fact that you do not have the luxury of continued immaturity. All that you have developed unto yourself in the fields of education, understanding, love, and womanhood, you must now use to make an uncertain situation, certain! Thomas included.

Send me all current information on Thomas. I will be obtaining funds this week and,

```
therefore, I shall call you then. I love you
princess. I truly believe in your abilities.
Try to suppress your fears and closely
follow your heart. It will be your guide to
safer pastures. You know that I have your
back either way that it goes down.

             I command the expressions
                      of your divinity,
                                    DAD
```

I was reminiscing here on Imani's visit early on in my incarceration. Grandma Shirley brought her. It was one of those terrible moments when I realized just how much my choices had affected those I loved. You get so caught up in the life, the streets, making money, that you forget about other people. Or you tell yourself you're doing that stuff *for* those other people, and still you forget about them. Then you get arrested, put in jail, and you are with other men who are in the same position. And it seems kind of normal, like part of the growing process or something. But then someone you love so much, your child, walks into the visitors' room and that veil of selfishness lifts. You see just how much you've hurt her. She needed a father then, and she needed one when she found out she was pregnant. And all I could do was write her a few words of encouragement.

This letter is written almost exactly one year after I was writing Le'mia about *her* pregnancy. Now I am trying to counsel Imani on hers. I felt so many different things at those times: regret, anger, frustration. But most of all, I felt a need to take a strong stand. I wanted to be a father, a man they could talk to – even if it was from prison. And I wanted to warn them to get it together and be parents to their children, no matter the circumstances. I knew from multiple experiences what it looked like when people didn't take that job seriously.

The man named Thomas referenced in this letter came to see me once, in USP Hazelton, West Virginia. That's how we met. He was solid – it seemed the two of them might just make it. My statement about "either way it goes down" was geared toward the possibility of Thomas not being there. In the end, Imani had my granddaughter, Amarah – and Thomas is still in the picture.

Knowing history

(Behind the scene)

Le-mia, my eldest child, and college grad, firmly expressed to me that Condoleezza Rice (former Secretary of State 2005-2009) was her role model and that her mother and I was not qualified because of our current social and personal status.

At the behest of being personally and socially offended, I reasoned that an essay entailing a frame of reference was imperative.

April 26, 2013

Le'mia,

Before I offer this spiel, it is important that I offer clarity for my point of view and reasons for such. It is never my intention to either offend, defame, or negate you. As a father who loves you universally, in depth, and painfully, I educate myself, in a factual sense, in order to offer assistance in your growth and development. Where I once failed you, I now render advice onto you.

A short story is a parable that shows why I see and say things about the way things are; In a village in Kenya, which is part of Africa, a boy of 13 years of age was killed by a lion. The whole village painfully mourned the loss. The father of the boy was the most skilled hunter in the village. He made an oath to rid the village of the vicious lion that had killed his son and also was killing their livestock at will.

A young boy from the village asked the hunter if he could accompany him on the hunt. The elders of the village informed the boy that it was too dangerous but, with strong and confident pleas, he won them over. After 24 hours of hunting, the boy, along with the skilled hunter found the lion. It was resting under a shade tree. The boy expected the hunter and him to pounce immediately upon the lion and kill it. Instead, they tracked the lion for three days and came to understand the lion's very nature. It was understood that the lion did what it did in order to survive. It did not do so out of hate or malice but rather through the necessity of survival.

Le'mia, it is necessary for your survival that you truly understand the nature of Western society as a whole. Though I will offer my autodidact analysis, how you use it lies at your feet as an opportunity and not on your back as a burden.

In order to fully grasp our (Black people) place in America, with its' politics, education, economics, religion, culture, etc…, you must first view our origins in America. It began with slavery, which was real, and claimed an estimated 200,000,000 people as victims. This is nearly a quarter of a billion people! This surpasses the 6 million victims of the Jewish holocaust by hundreds of millions. There is and never has existed any greater human atrocity. We arrived as human cargo in Massachusetts and Virginia. One of the first things to happen to the new arrivals was the removal of their cultural awareness. The newly enslaved were forbidden from practicing any form of their cultural spirituality. It was replaced with pagan rituals. Also forbidden was the use of their native tongues. It was replaced with English so that it would always be known what was being said. Families were separated from one another. Mother from child, husband from wife, aunt from niece, nephew from uncle, and so on and so forth. These kind of things removed any chance of a united revolt and this terrorization continued on for centuries leaving as a result, a broken disenfranchised people.

Slavery was even justified by the U.S. Constitution itself, stating that Africans were 3/5 of a man and subject to ownership. We were never written in to the Constitution to integrate America.

Now, look at how the enslaved have allegedly become free…

The Civil War was a politically motivated war having nothing to do with Blacks. The Northern Republicans, who were coined with the name "Yankees", were at odds with their southern neighbors who were called "Confederates". The South, which relied heavily upon the paradigm represented by free slave labor was opposed to any idea that would change this model. It was not that the North wanted to abolish slavery and liberate those enslaved but simply wanted a united economic system that would achieve greater independence from mother England which, at that time, was the strongest country in the world. War ensued. The North was in a bitter battle with the South and was in great fear of losing. The bigot Republican president, Abraham Lincoln, saw one option. Free the slaves. Tell them, if they fought for their freedom on the front lines, they would earn their freedom. The freeing of the slave was a strategic military action. The famous term, Buffalo Soldier", was derived from this decision.

The vicious republican, Abraham Lincoln later wrote; "If there existed any option that granted military success other than freeing the slaves, then I would have hastily done so. I never intended to remove anyone's property". The bigot was later shot and killed by John Wilkes Booth.

Now, let's review the economic, educational, political and other systems that the severely ignorant and disenfranchised slaves inherited.

America is founded on three (3) economic worldly functions; Imperialism, Capitalism, and Socialism.

As defined by Webster's dictionary... Imperialism is; (1) of or relating to an empire, emperor, or empress. (2) designating a nation or government holding sovereign rights over colonies or dependency's. My insight is that imperialism simply means one power, one word, one law… In other words, a Kingdom. When they say colonies, think of the founding of the original 13 colonies of early America. These are now called states and 50 of them exist in addition to 3 U.S. territories. An imperial government controls all the assets of said Kingdom/Nation. The masses are grouped by status or class, ie; upper, middle, lower. or, viewed in terms of a hierarchy; royalty, servants, peasants. Imperialism thrives on the paradigms of capitalism and socialism alike. This ensures wealth, power, and the supremacy of the imperialist.

Capitalism, as defined by Webster's dictionary… (1) an economic system in which the means of production and distribution are privately owned and operated for profit. I state that capitalism is referred to as the competitive market or, private sector. It places its' citizens at each others throats in order to produce and distribute, for profit, consumer goods with no regard for individual morality or humanity. This competition for what little revenue the imperial hierarchy is willing to allow, as retainable by individuals, is fought over at the exploitation of the poor and powerless. Most billionaires derive their wealth from the capitalist private sector and yet, indirectly surrender all their capitalist gain to the State/Empire.

Socialism is defined by Webster's dictionary as… (1) a theory or system of ownership of the means of production by society, rather than by individuals. Socialism, where it pertains to us, means that all production and distribution is controlled by society, except society in this case, does not mean the people. It stands for the government because it is upheld in Western dogma that the people appoint the government. This is called the industrial sector. It is a place where unions contract out labor forces in mass amounts, subjecting them to industrial servitude. Yet, the possession of imperial wealth never shifts resulting in further imperial control of the economic paradigm while appeasing the thirst of the people.

Such an economic structure was never founded for the economic success of the ordinary citizen. It does, however, ensure a lifetime of servitude by removing the chances for success. The economic system of America was intentionally designed to exploit and stagnate the Black masses. Do your research on sharecropping, which was implemented after slavery was abolished in order to support the legal exploitation of the allegedly free man.

Politics is defined by Webster's dictionary as… (1) the science and art of government. (2) political tactics and methods. (3) factional scheming for power. Politics is the artistic science of diabolical power thrusting. It is used against the people/citizens to perpetuate control by the elite. The world elite is believed to be 7% of the global population. Yet, only 1% of that 7% is privy to the secret workings of the political mechanism.

Moreover, this 1% creates, dictates, and strategically calculates the precise movement of the political agenda.

There are several forms of political structures. Empires/Kingdoms, Dictatorships, Communism, Socialism, Capitalism, Democracies, Republics, etc…

America is belived to practice the hypocrisy of democracy. In this, you will find 4-5 political sects. However, the first two U.S. presidents were federalists. This means that they supported a government in which individual states unite at national level but remain independent in their own internal affairs. Under the federalist government we were slaves. There was a political party called the Whig party that existed in the mid 1800's. 3 U.S. presidents came from the Whig party, one of them being Abraham Lincoln. He later founded the Republican Party in 1856. The Independent party had one U.S. president, John Quincy Adams. This party shared no political views with any other party or supporters and chose to govern as they seen fit. The Democrats, of which there have been 17 U.S. presidents, including Obama, expound the popular rhetoric that government is run by the people through the election of representatives... HOAX! The Republicans, of which there have been 21 U.S. presidents, believe in an ideal form of democracy that is centered around wealth.

Today, there are liberals. They believe in traditional American government. There are conservatives, with origins in the British Conservative Party, who believe in the conservation of imperial wealth and power.

Contrary to popular belief, the majority of the allegedly newly freed slaves were republicans. History shows that the Black man voted republican in the late 1800's through the early to mid 1900's. The north, which was coined with the label of "free states", were republican states, and the Black man voted as republicans. The republican bigot, Abraham Lincoln, was quoted after the signing of the Emancipation Proclamation, verbatim; "The freeing of the slaves was a military necessity, absolutely essential to the Union". He further stated; "If I could save the Union without freeing the slaves, then I would do it. If I could save it by freeing the slaves, I would do it. And, if I could do it by freeing some, and leaving others alone, I would do it".

The freeing of the slaves was a military action designed to save the Union. The Black man fanactically supported the republican party until it began to sell out to the south when Herbert Hoover and Calvin Coolidge were President. This started the dependent Black love affair with the Democratic Party, which came to the rescue during the time when Black southerners were being lynced, raped, murdered, and maimed by the sadistic KKK. Despite this, there is no political mechanism in Western society that is designed for the betterment of the Black man. Only [R]evolution.

Every political party in the history of the U.S. was designed to stagnate, negate, exploit, and exterminate the Black man. Always remember that we were in chains when each one of these parties were established. All saw those chains as politically correct and none of the parties were founded with us in mind. It can be said that one would suffer from a severe case of acute delusion if they attempted to identify with any U.S. political party. Even with a Black First Family in the White House, we are no better off than we were when we first arrived, in chains, at Plymouth, Massachusetts. It is commonly said that the Black American's problem is with society's political agenda. Look at affirmative action, welfare, project housing, public schooling, WIC food programs, etc.... We are viewed as politically dispensable.

Education is defined by Webster's dictionary as... (1) the process of educating. (2) knowledge, etc. thus to to develop. (3) formal schooling. My conscious opinion is that education is the cultivation of the unique intuition, inquisitiveness, curiosity, and divine desire to know. In turn, this is nurtured by elders and teachers for the development of universal knowledge and higher learning in all fields of life. This nourishment of the quest to become learned, birthed the great minds and extraordinary hoteps (one who has acquired supreme knowledge) of ancient Africa. This process of educating should be unbiased and limitless in coverage. It should always be the intent of the educator to spare no subject matter so that a vast teaching is retained by the pupil.

Now, let's review the origins of education so that we can understand where I am going with this spiel.

Beyond a shadow of a doubt, history shows that civilization and education originated in Africa. Before the rise of the Egyptian there existed 27 dynasties. Each of these dynasties thrived for an average of 300 years and it is commonly believed that they may have spanned a total of 30,000 years. Following these dynasties came the Egyptian empire which marked the great decline of the previous civilization. The egyptians created the greatest ancient archives in history. The Library of Alexandria was where the study of mathematics, science, medicine. stone masonry, agriculture, written text, art, earthenware, etc. was compiled and stored.

Such Africans as Imhotep, Orisis, Hannibal, etc., were upheld as Gods by the new coming of uncivilized foreigners. These men possessed an education and wisdom, from within a cultivated Kingdom. The uncivilized foreigners were awestruck. It was here that the uncivilized realized their inferiority when compared to the supremely educated and civilized epitome of man and, in reponse, the idea of using education as a weapon was born.

As quoted by Joseph Stalin; "Education is a weapon, whose effect depends on who holds it in his hands, and whom it is aimed". I concur with this statement.

Remember that the Library of Alexandria was later destroyed by these uncivilized conquerors. Ancient Egyptian art, text, and educational artifacts can now be found in museums on every continent. This fact resulted from the cultural robbery of the first, longest, and greatest civilized educational system in the history of the world.

Most learned people know that a people without a history and an education, is a people without a future. Western civilization weaponized education once they garnered control of it. Consider this... you can acquire a P.H.D. in any Western field of study. The belief is that, as a result, you will receive a career, which in turn, will guarantee employment. Well, this one-sided view of education entraps the victim of this weapon to a lifetime of servitude. It means that you cannot retire until you have worked for at least 30 years, or sometimes not until you reach the age of 72. Yet, outside of your field of study, your degree is obsolete. A brain surgeon cannot work as a mechanic, nor can a rocket scientist be employed as a dentist, or a bank executive work as a carpenter. That is, unless you learn the trade. It is the design of Western education to teach you one field so that you will always serve in that one field. Remember after the alleged recession, hundreds of thousands of well educated Ivy League graduates were left unemployed. They lacked the education to integrate into other available fields.

Education is a political weapon (Brown vs. The Board of Education), as well as being an instrument of economic exploitation. If one simply relies on the present system of education to educate them, they will be victimized by this weaponry. Thirty years and a lifetime of servitude under the guise of a career title. I conclude, it is important to identify the weapons that are, and were, systematically used to create the state of Black America.

Le'mia, don't regret, redeem. Realize and repair. Become the autodidact person that you must become. Broaden your studies. Rely on no one and question everything. Prove all subject matters thyself. Yet, utilize academic America 100%. Your education is yours when learned and taught by your own self.

My beloved daughter, it will be a fatal injustice to my soul if I neglect to spew my pride of you. But the word pride robs my feelings of its' true impact. Where, as your father loves you, I live you. I surrender my life to you. Become, at your age, what I did not, the embodiment of greatness. I will utilize all of my life's energy to perpetuate your essence. You are startlingly intriguing. Suffice it to write, I am at your mercy. Great admiration.

                      I bid your immaculateness,
                                      Father

I wish I could remember where that lion parable came from, but it really stood out as a great metaphor to explain to my daughter why I was telling her everything. I wish someone had sat me down and told me some stories from this country's history – the ones they didn't tell you in the classroom. At that time, in prison, I was reading so many books about American history, the Civil War, and the like. Howard Zinn's *A People's History of the United States* was a favorite. It made me mad, how much wasn't taught to me, and I really wanted to give that information to my daughter, ready or not.

This letter was kind of a rebuttal to a prior statement that she had made to me. At some point during her schooling at Prairie View she began to identify certain African Americans as being heroic figures in her life. This is so often how Black history gets taught, with a few iconic people representing all the work that so many Black people you never heard of did. One person she became interested in was Condoleezza Rice, who had been Secretary of State under President George W. Bush. Rice was representing the Republican party by that time. At some point, my daughter had stated that her mother and I were disappointing figures in her life in comparison to such African Americans as Rice. I was livid. So this is part of my rebuttal that I put together (I actually sent her an essay which is even longer than the letter included here). It was not to directly criticize her admiration of Ms. Rice, but to clarify the foundation on which Ms. Rice stood – the Republican party. That is the reason I mention President Lincoln, a famous Republican, over and over. Le'mia definitely thinks I'm crazy sometimes because of the way I go about saying things, but she never says I'm boring!

(Behind the scene)

I have experienced firsthand the nefarious meanings of mental, spiritual, physical, and emotional cannibalism. To eat the genetic make-up and existence of your very own children through an unstable lifestyle is an act of grave altruism.

I was loving my words that day when I wrote about the "nefarious meanings" of "cannibalism". What I was trying to say was I felt like an assailant of my own kids. Before I could finally protect them from the world – which is what so much of these letters are about – I had to come to terms with the fact that I had destroyed things in them. I had eaten up their spirituality, their emotional, mental, and physical health, with my choices and actions. Like a cannibal, eating one's own. That made me feel horrible and I was trying to do something to reverse the flow.

Boys and girls

November 20, 2013

My Dearest Reasons*,

My reasons, with whom I share my physical features and genetic code, I, your humbled patriarch, ask you for your forgiveness. I offer no offensive assertions, nor do I perpetuate excuses for my historically sore immaturities. I only render onto you my reasons.

Le'mia, my dearest first born, pure child, and elegant woman. I always anticipate, with pleasure, seeing the projection of your soulful demeanor. You never knew that the idea of your birth began the process of my life's appraisal. I would have never intentionally adopted practices of neglectful parenting. Looking back now, I realize that this wasn't me. It was surely He, trying to find the prudence in me.

Your strongest attribute remains your profound sensitivity. I knew this the very first time you looked into me. I now know that I was completely off course. I am now assured on how to cultivate my life[1]s most greatest resource.

Imani, my dearest faith, my rebel. Vibrant child and revolutionary woman. You hold the same gravity as breath to my existence. The first time that we were face to face, you placed those piercing eyes on me and I knew exactly what you were trying to convey. I miss these kinds of moments that kept the rest of the world in abeyance. As for my grandchild, nurture her with an abundance of love and respect. Make her your earnest duty and turn her into the priceless diamond that is a reflection of you.

Maurice Jr., my dearest conqueror of defined tribulations, like me in misfortune, truly an admired man-child. I agree with all those feelings that you struggle with concerning me. It is however, the continuation of a cycle that direly lacks in the expressions of manliness. This cycle which I write about, is the same that ravaged the spirit of my father and my inability to be free. Overcome my son and be as I've instructed you in the past… Be the cycle breaker. Be the strength that makes our bloodline once again chaste. Though the inheritance of that struggle too may be your only reward, cling firmly to your inherited spirit of a warrior to combat these unfavorable discords.

Demetrius, my dearest physical reflection, my unintended nemesis. Your disjointed affiliations concerning myself have proved to be valid. Your mixed emotions about me are totally accepted. Our kinship started with accumulated controversy, in which you played no role. The controversy was mine, reacting off perceptions of stories never told. Obviously, I did nothing to seek out the value that sat within you. I only saw my struggle, while misunderstanding that you were also feeling the wrath of that struggle. Forgive me, my son, for all that you have had to endure in my absence. No excuses, you are my reason for placing my reasons within common sense.

I conclude that all of you need to practice your right to individuality in all endeavors. Let the first law of life's journey command you to recognize the perfection in yourself. You are greater than an idea. You are more concise than a theory. You are individualized in a material essence that is beyond anyone's selfish indoctrination. It is within you that the depth of in depth though is reached... You have the ability to be a critically thinking, critically reasoning and ever evolving human paragon...

I bid your immaculateness,
Father

* A letter addressing the author's children

My sons and I have had a harder time connecting than me and my daughters. Demetrius is my nemesis in ways – we battle a lot. He's working in the music business right now. He wants his own identity but, instead, he's always being told he's just like his dad. It doesn't help that we look so much alike. His mother and I had a rocky relationship; I wanted her to get an abortion when she was pregnant with him. But honestly, she was 'the one' as far as I'm concerned, if only I had been a little more mature.

Maurice, Jr. is like me, in too many ways. He's following in my footsteps – mental instability, criminality, incarceration. Going down *that* road. He is incarcerated right now and I don't even know where he is – he hasn't reached out to me. But when he's not drugging, high, and feeling malicious, he is his beautiful self. He loves his child and truly wants the best for all people.

This social condition is bigger than just my own children. Most parents choose to only think about their own child's situation when things are bad. But research shows that, in this case, there is a bigger issue that needs to get cleaned up. Because without proper context, you burn out. You just keep trying to solve the problem in front of you – like your kid's issues – and ignore the bigger problem which could end up solving humanity's problems. Poor people have more of these problems, and poor people don't always think they are valuable or impactful enough to solve them because that is what we are told, in so many ways. We just stay on the hamster wheel, trying to attend to those closest to us while the world spins faster and faster under our feet.

In a way, I am sacrificing my kids for a greater good, learning from my experiences as a child – and then a parent – raised up in this condition. Now I try to teach my people how to get out of this condition – like by writing this book. I definitely have to take the heat for my kids' troubles, but I want to take the heat for my people, too. I sometimes wonder if this is the kind of experience that prophets have, having that call on them to connect people together for a common cause. I am not saying I *am* a prophet, it just feels like I'm saying something a lot of people don't want to hear, but I say it anyway. I am someone who knows things through life's experiences, and I feel called to teach others those lessons. After all, Black people have done that for me in my past, for all of us. At the end of the day, those are the people I wish my kids were learning about in school, the true icons.

April 1, 2014

Demetrius,

I offer a stern congrats on your recent obtainment of employment, for any and all accomplishments garnered in the direction of growth, and development is an advancement for both, yourself and the betterment of our family. Therefore, it is my humble obligation to acknowledge your honorable efforts.

Soon, I will address the matter in your previous letter to me in due course. But, first, I must elaborate on its emotional content.

Your letter was enriched with master contemplation and sound reasoning. A tribute to tedious struggling and meticulous self-evaluation, which led to an increased desire to express yourself.

Know that I did not admonish you out of pure spitefulness, or fault-finding. But, me acting in accordance with the laws set in place that governs the essentials of our manhood. While the solid framework of our manhood was established long before the birth of you and I, it still remains utterly important that we maintain its robustness, and stay its righteous course. Worth noting here also is, the identity, dignity, and integrity of our ancestor's sacrifices, which must be preserved in our hearts and actions to solidify the family's structure for future contemplating.

By all means, I only seek to assist you in the strengthening of your manly development as I see fit. It is always an enlightening privilege to correspond with you. You and I have much to learn and teach each other. Know that all which I possess in experience, and thought is already rightfully yours. therefore, make haste in receiving your jewels.

I love you Son, and fare you in wellness....

Father

The matter I mention "in your previous letter" was about manhood and it gets addressed here. Demetrius had begun to act out angrily toward women – like nieces, girlfriends, and aunts. I was reminding him to control himself, that our responsibility as men is to protect women. You can't protect them and harm them at the same time. That is unmanly, and something I feel very strongly about. I bring it up in a lot of my letters, trying to teach my sons – or counsel my sisters – on the responsibilities of men. My son's actions are partly on me, of course, because anger and violence get passed down through generations; my dad beat his wife, and so it went on down the line. I wanted my son to be better than his history, to break the cycle.

April 3, 2014

Le'mia,

Supreme admiration Princess, and an abundance of love which I project upon the entirety of your essence.

Please, forgive the untimely response to your previous correspondence. Between my critical responsibility to rehabilitation in light of the surgery, and my tedious duty to the projects which I'm currently engaged, time is rendered quite mismanageable these days.

Thank you, for the meaningful card expressing Father's Day. There aren't many cards that express in them exactly what one truly intends to convey. Though, your thoughts are telegraphed through the distinction of your beautiful behavior, I nevertheless felt the genuineness of what you intended via card, to convey to me. Again, thank you, and let us continue to work towards the strengthening of our father and daughter lineal covenant.

You stated in your recent letter that you were becoming frustrated with the teaching duties which you now hold employment thereof. But, if you were to place all of the general components of the situation into its proper perspective, then your frustration has a suitable notation. Take note that your characteristic as a natural educator are linked with, that of your situation entails that you educate pupils who are sustaining a disenfranchised status, within a system (juvenile detention), which operates in a storm of red-tape. And, the hardest part of educating anyone is, having to do it through the confinements of a particular science.

In the future, before entering into an institution of learning, first observe the methods of how long and with who, this institution is attempting to educate. This scrutinizing tactic is very important for the pure educator, and highly necessary for the minds that are innocent in the receptiveness of being educated. Though all are well-intended, any misapprehension of these relations can allot the miscarriage of an entire society.

On the surface, the necessity of the implementation of a substantial education can appear quite trivial. If you were to tell someone that an education is unbalanced, or made to be weaponized intentionally, they would probably view you as a person of dear insanity. How an individual, or group are educated is paramount on the significance of that individual, or groups' position in society, or global stage. As in your case, these realistic disparities have a gargantuan effect on the life of an educator. They (you), are left to bridge the gap which gives appropriate nutriments to the needs of the pupil, while also maintaining a stealth-like posture in the navigation of being loyal to that of their assigned appointers (the system).

Obviously, this is absolutely no easy task, and its failure, or success has the potential of grave consequences. A breakdown of an individual, or group, can render a breakdown of a system, which by their nature can perpetuate the breakdown of an entire nation. This, you are bearing witness to in our society at this very moment.

In reference to the specific system which you are charged with giving the appropriate nutriments to the needs of its agents… First, I will quote a statement that was made by Ms. Iyanla Vanzant, author, T.V. personality, etc., "The moment in which I cease in my learning, will be the moment I am no longer fit to teach."

Learn of these innocent children, and what are the mechanisms that hinders their ability to overcome adverse behaviors. Cut the red tape, at least in the confinement of your very own mind if not any further. You may recognize that it is the same attempt at abandonment which you are suggesting that has normalized their present outlook on life. Remember, as you were also, they are the true victims, not your present state of mind. Do not bring forth any additional failures to their lives by injecting your version of intolerance to an already condition of instability.

However, the fact still remains that, you skillfully and characteristically possess the experience needed to cure their illnesses. And, I believe you understand why. Of course, you are them, made matured. The wicked head of disfunction which has ravaged the framework of your very own life has appeared with its unbiased injustices to do the exact same thing unto them.

Now, spiritually, and mentally, revert back into the attentiveness of your heart. Rely upon the initial reason why you chose to enter the field of education, specifically, the educating of children with special needs. Focus yourself back onto the love in your heart which propelled you to a connection in the beginning. Learn the depths of what is truly ailing them, for this will lead to the path that highlights the proper way of understanding what methods must be implemented to obtain the reality of a healthy child.

Question: What distinguishes a great educator from an educator with a job? Ill be waiting impatiently for your response. Please, be well.

Sincerely,
Father

Le'Mia was teaching in a juvenile delinquent institution, the Youth Services Center in Washington, DC. It's where they detain incarcerated juveniles on pretrial – young folks awaiting trial or sentencing before being transferred to a higher security institution. I was proud of her for doing that. It also got me looking back on my own educational experience, from the perspective of a teacher like her. I got to wondering how my teachers could have made things better for us. I realize that many of them had no idea who they were teaching; my peers and I came from a world some of those teachers never knew. And that would still be okay, if they had been willing to learn something about us and our lives at that moment. But you can't teach a kid from the DC projects in the same way you teach someone at a Georgetown charter school. And some of my teachers, well, they did know the neighborhood. But they were trying to forget where they came from. That was destructive for us and for them.

My daughter was feeling frustrated in her position, and I believed that if she considered who the students in front of her really were she might be able to communicate more effectively with them. That meant she would have to look at herself, where she came from, who she was – and who she had become. She could understand these kids better than she thought and then be a role model for them. If I had a few more teachers who *really* saw me, I might have avoided some of those things I chose to do in my life. I knew my daughter could be a "great educator" and not just "an educator with a job", but it would take some work. That was something that a lot of teachers were unwilling to partake in.

```
May 30, 2014

Demetrius,

It's my honor to make known my regard for
you, supreme regard, as I respect your
status within the nucleus of family.

The purpose of this letter is to inform you
that, it is of noble need that I retain the
full extent of your focus.

One of the most unadaptable things about being
imprisoned is the lack of ability to see the
```

world directly. It is exigent that I have a visible vessel to the world at large, and its intriguing multi-diverse expressions. By maintaining a strong and vigilant mind in all which you will encounter throughout the day, you can offer me the data which I will need to fulfill this noble need. I too require accurate information so that I may have an opportunity to develop sound reasoning when pro-jecting an educational duty unto the minds of your siblings, and yourself. Process everything with the rationale of your very own definition, and interpret its legitimate findings to me.

This, my son, is a part of the eternal living process which all men must seek to utilize. By keeping the ecology of you, and I intact, we will preserve the continuation of our noble obligations to our culture family, and our human family alike.

I beseech that you pay your dues diligently. Make it a remarkable habit to incorporate a philosophical vision within the senses of your nature.

Respond at your earliest convenience. Please, be well.

Father

Parenting different

I depended on letters from my children for many reasons. One was to get a look at the world that was cut off to me. Only through their eyes and words could I see what was happening out there. Really happening. Not just the news headlines, but what people were feeling and, more importantly, what my kids were feeling and why.

My letters to them were reinforcements and encouragements. They were teachings after listenings. In a weird way, it was an ideal situation for parenting; a kid can't interrupt a letter, they can't defend themselves to a piece of paper or an email. So hopefully they just listened, and thought, and processed. This can build a strong connection, even when the correspondents are far away from each other. I enjoyed this act of parenting through writing and took advantage of it to share my thoughts – and to have their thoughts shared with me. Now, some might think that a man serving time in prison for murder might not have anything to offer his children. They would be wrong. My life experiences, coupled with my intellectual, spiritual, and humanistic outlook, can offer a lot to a young person. I believe, no matter all the bad things I have done in the past, that my life is useful as information for the future of my children. They are big reasons for me staying on track now, and for working to make this world different from what it is at this moment.

Co-author's note

Over 1.1 million African American men were in prison in the United States as of February 2023. Approximately 500,000 of them were fathers. Many of their fathers also served time and studies show it is likely that many of their sons will serve time as well. A recent study out of Florida Atlantic University's College of Social Work and Criminal Justice noted: "the data shows that more fathers, sons, and grandfathers are being incarcerated at the same time, and also supports research indicating that children with a parent in jail or prison are five to six times more likely to become offenders". This is borne out in Maurice's experience; his father served a thirty-day furloughed incarceration for domestic abuse. (The terms of furlough were that he was allowed to leave the prison for eight hours a day for work, and then return. He was unable to leave on weekends). Maurice, Jr. is incarcerated at the time of this writing.

The above-mentioned study also shows the ways that incarceration impedes so many fathers from parenting, something that Maurice and others work hard to overcome from inside of prison. Sometimes the impediment comes in the form of mothers and maternal families deciding that incarcerated fathers are not fit for continued contact with their children. Participants of the study explained that these family members attempted to turn their children against them in such a way that even upon their release there was no relationship between father and child. There is a feeling of powerlessness that can come from being an incarcerated parent, as confirmed through Maurice's words, as well as the data-driven research.

In the larger discussion of absent Black fathers, the economic effects are often emphasized. Stereotypes, and conflating money with care, help characterize many Black men as lacking empathy for their families. But this accusation ignores some of the ways in which Black fathers continue to contribute even while not financially providing or living in the home. In fact, African American fathers "are more likely to be in contact with their children than any other ethnic or racial group", according to research cited in the abovementioned study. These fathers can still play an important role in their children's lives, their presence often linked to less "deviant" behavior in their children. In addition, the authors of the study write:

> Much of the dialogue regarding African American fathers has neglected to address the root cause of why so many of them are absent from their children's lives. Instead, many [leaders] have used their political and social platforms to ask, "Where are African American fathers?" This deflects from the harsh reality that many are in jail or prison due to historical, cultural, and structural oppression. Despite the overwhelmingly negative image of fatherhood, many African American men play an active role in their children's lives, even if they do not live in the same household. However, as this study showed, the incarceration cycle will continue as long as society continues to hold them in a psychological and physical prison that disrupts caregiving, perpetuates stigma, destroys paternal bonds, and complicates reentry processes.

We see this research pointing to the conditions that Maurice writes about, those of "historical, cultural, and structural oppression". This study (among others) argues what many already know: incarceration can obliterate Black families. And it confirms that – for those who have them – fathers, whether in prison or out, are important to the growth of their children, and to the family unit at large. Children in this study also showed that having a relationship with their father, in one form or another, provided a sense of security and comfort that was missing when no relationship existed at all.[2]

As is apparent in Maurice's case, fathers generally want connection with their children and believe it to be their right, no matter their past. One can find reams of research confirming the importance of supporting and encouraging parental relationships from inside of prison so that, once a parent is released, there is a foundation upon which to build.

When I went to prison, my children were young. However, prior to incarceration I had already established some degree of a bond with all of them except Quion. Up until that point, I had only laid eyes on Quion once. His mother's parents were very strict and wouldn't allow me to visit him, or him me. Honestly, I don't know if it was solely about who I was – or wasn't – or about the fact that his mother had gotten pregnant at such a young age while living under their care. Nonetheless, his mother continued to put distance between us long after she had moved out to live on her own. The only reason, according to her, that she even reached out to me while I was incarcerated was because Quion became more persistent in questioning who his father was. I have to give her credit for that.

During my years of incarceration, one of the hardest reality checks to get through was the attitude shifts from my family and friends. To become estranged by people who knew you outside of your crime seemed unimaginable to me. I didn't expect that all they would see in me now was my crime – as if I was suddenly not the person they had loved or cared about before.

Though the rejection from Quion's mother and family started prior to prison, I wasn't mentally prepared for the continual judgment by his mother. It felt like she had become possessed or something, it was so sudden and surprising.

Only much later did I find out that all of that wasn't really about me; it was more about how the family of Quion's mother wanted to represent to society. I guess it wasn't a good look to have a felon in the family. Society has a lot to say about incarcerated people, even though our penal system is supposedly about people doing their time, rehabilitating, and then returning to humanity a better person. A lot of people don't believe that's possible. The bottom line is that it's a helpless feeling trying to grasp at relationships from inside of a prison, trying to communicate and continue on with people you were once close to. I really don't recommend it.

4
Cousins, comrades, cellies, friends, and teachers

November 20, 2010

Talib*,

As is the custom in the credo of Islam, I greet you in the Arabic language by saying, as-salaamu-alaikum.

The letter and photo that you sent to me was received in gratitude. The young lady, and yourself, are truly a pair of beautiful human beings. It is refreshing seeing you both taking advantage of the pleasures that Allah has made available to mankind for their relaxational needs. May the moment arrive when both you and I together will be afforded an opportunity to enjoy such an availability, Insha' Allah.

The photo is a clear piece of evidence that conveys what I have been trying to explain to you for quite some time now. It is a recognition of our past experiences being made right. For us, it becomes imperative that our future be filled with the discipline of good standards, as well as understanding the obligations to the people in our lives.

This blueprint will become comprehensive through the instructions of Allah according to the teachings of your belief, the Qur'an and Sunnah of the rasool. Then your obligations to the world, humanity, and self should be implemented in direct accordance with that for which you are instructed from. By all means we both shared, in previous days, the excuse that the sound instructions of our spiritual teachings were not understood by us. But now, we surely cannot share such an excuse.

In reference to your current issues with the nature of women, my opinion is that most of our women are out of alignment with their true nature simply because, we men are profoundly out of alignment with ours. It appears that the more women share our dominate space in the world the more the velocity of our strength as men weakens. Why?

What is now being highlighted, from our earthly counterpart, is the fact that women possess divine attributes that just cannot be matched by the divine attributes of men. Her place within our space is becoming more absolute and apparent. Both of our divine natures, though, bear their finest fruits when we are not in conflict, but rather, in complete harmony with one another. It is becoming more understood that we are not simply created to procreate. We must also be willing to sustain the mental, and spiritual balance that's connected to our physical being. This is a necessary process. And, we must spend the time and energy defining, loving, and nurturing that process.

Wa-alaikum-salaam,
Cousin

* Author's cousin

Father figures

My two cousins, Talib and Eric, are from my dad's side of the family. The three of us really didn't have fathers in our lives much, so we sort of acted like each other's dad. Eric took on that role for me, and then I pretty much raised my cousin, Talib – he is eight years younger. Talib had been locked up before me but had just gotten out at the time of this letter. I really wanted him to hold on to some of those hard lessons we learned inside; I wanted him to stay with that Islamic thinking. I believed that would help him on the outside.

In this letter I am trying to speak to him in his own language, the language we shared in prison. I use the words of our faith when discussing life, values, and decision making. I was trying to get through to him as to where he needed to be, because he didn't sound like he was there from what he had written. For one thing he sent me a photograph of a woman he was seeing and referred to her as an "old head". This was unacceptable to me, on numerous levels. Obviously, for one thing, that is not a respectful thing to call your woman. I reminded him that the male/female relationship can't thrive if both partners are not living at their highest potential. If a woman is being made to feel low, then the connection won't be strong between them – that high potential is lost.

The way Talib referenced the woman in the picture also made me wonder if he had other women, other 'categories'. Like an old one, a young one, one with a job, maybe one that was just fun to get with. Something was not right with how he was presenting his affections, and I needed to get to where his thoughts were.

The Qur'an, the holy book of Islam, holds powerful teachings about discipline. These are very relevant and useful to the incarcerated. Muslims declare one God and acknowledge Muhammad as God's messenger. Muslims learn about the values of prayer and fasting and giving ourselves to help our fellow man. These are perspectives that a lot of us weren't exposed to when we were coming up. Through our study together, Islam really seemed to strengthen Talib and I wanted his strength to continue now that he was facing the outside world, filled with so many distractions and impurities. He had a blueprint, as I called it, and I didn't want him to forget that. He had the rule book already. I think the reason why so many of us made so many mistakes in our lives is because we never had a rule book. Or, at least, the rules that we learned didn't have much to do with lifting up humankind. I felt I had a responsibility to remind my cousin of all of this. After all, I was his brother in Islam – and the backup father.

January 16, 2011

Eric*,

May the genuineness of this scribe find you with a sincere mind, and the inquisitiveness to acquire information.

I am truly intrigued by the stability of your unstudied wits. I also identify you as being yet another remarkable human being.

I sat in meditation today and reflected on the correspondence that I received from you on Sunday. I concluded that you are well informed of your manly obligations to our family and the necessity with which they should be sustained. What muddles me the most, however, is why you have been driven to the point of using so much energy to deliberately hinder yourself from benefiting from life's most suitable undertakings.

In my humble opinion, you are far more deserving of a life that is better than the one you have chosen to adopt. Among the individuals in your isolated peer group, you have demonstrated more of a competent outlook concerning the basic applications of life skills. The self affliction that you have rendered on to yourself through the degradation of debasement provides a unique sign that you must begin to again harmonize yourself so that you are realigned with the true authorities of your manliness.

Whomever accepts a system of particular thoughts must also be aware that systematic thought processes need to have a direct alliance with the Creator (Creative Forces), the universe, and universal mankind. Therefore, before any such system(s) can render themselves in harmony with reality, you must first know the fundamentals of your own person. Who you are and what you are have to be defined by you.

This definition becomes much more realistic when observed in a humanitarian context such as: We are the Homo Sapien Sapiens of the human race. We are greater than the idea that we are, more concise than the theory that we project, interdependent upon one another, yet individualized in material essence beyond any doctrine. It is within us that the real depth of our deepest thoughts are reached. We are the critical thinking, critical reasoning, and ever evolving species on this planet we call Earth.

Eric, we shall meet in the physical sense and connect deeper in the spiritual sense. It is the duty of men to sit and plan for the future of their family's path, as well as their own. This engagement is far overdue, so we must act in accordance with its' necessity.

Give my highest of regards to our bloodline.

I Bid You In Consciousness,
Maurice

* Author's first cousin

March 10, 2013

Eric,

This continues the synopsis that I previously wrote and conversed with you about. Greetings, and may this find you in a state of open mindedness and still with the acquisitiveness to acquire knowledge.

Recently we had a telephone conversation concerning your mother who was literally laboring herself into the ground, in spite of her not needing to do so. I admire, in the extreme, that which which you have found to be so displeasurable. These sorts of things are truly deserving of such an offensive inclination. She is the favorite of aunties amongst all of your cousins. That alone speaks in high volume as to what kind of individual she is. This laborious type of systematic thinking unmercifully plagues the lives of so many of our family and kind in race. It should be unfavorable to each of our following generations for what will be inherited by this back breaking slavery. The result will be nothing in the form of land, business, or financial inheritance, not to mention the massive torment that will riddle the mind, body, and spirit at the behest of decades of human misuse.

What kind of legitimate chance could she have had to avoid the life of hard laboring during those systematic battles that were being fought to overcome the view of not being seen as a people of rights equal to whites? The aftermath of Jim Crow, the upstart of the Civil Rights Movement, Affirmative Action, etc.. They all required the fighting of great battles, which were hard, and massive individual and collective laboring became the hallmark of fundamental thought and action for the people during that period in time. When these opportunities presented themselves, laboring three times harder than the average white American became the habitually vicious process that was passed down to generation after generation. The point is; she knows nothing further but to labor, and to labor continuously to survive, while also taking her rightful place within the American society... as this was the basis of the process.

Surely, our personal duties as kin, being displeased at the awareness of this reality requires us to act upon this displeasurement. The pressure that we have witnessed our grandmother, mothers, aunties, fathers, and ourselves suffer under was and is real. That thing within us that seems to be in constant conflict with our environment is real. I've learned, however, that we are the direct threats, or helpers, in this conflict. My dear cousin, in order that we may deal with the suffering of our family and the perpetuations of society, we must win the war which gives us the ability to master the circumspect of self. Complete self mastery!

Please send my regards to the family... I deploy a keen respect unto yourself.

Allow thought to suffice,
Maurice

My cousin Eric's mom is my aunt. We're blood. In the March 10th letter, I wanted him to know that I saw things the same way he did when it came to the subject of work and his mom.

His instincts were right on; hard work has to result in something great, otherwise it's just work for work's sake. Unfortunately, some people think that just working hard is the thing to do, no matter the results. Instead of analyzing what we are getting from the work, we just keep doing it, laboring hard, trying to show how committed we are to living the lives we dream of – but don't usually end up having. Eric noticed this in his mother, while I was noticing it taking place in Eric. My cousin is a good man, never been in trouble like me. He always kept his head down and worked. But he wasn't investing in anything – mind, body, spirit, or finances. How was he going to solidify a legacy, support his offspring, like that? He really had nothing to show for all his hard work, nothing that said, "you've been here". He had fallen into his mother's footsteps.

I could relate to this habit because I followed in my parents' footsteps, too. At one time I was drugged and diseased, just like them. Sometimes it can be hard to recognize that we're doing the exact same thing as our parents because it looks different in the modern world we are living in. We don't identify it as the same behavior. Eric might have been making more money than his mother, and able to buy a house in a neighborhood she was not able to at one time, but he was still working without any vision. Just like her.

With me, my mom didn't serve 20 years in prison but she did endure her own imprisonment, suffering from addiction and domestic violence. Both of us were drug addicts, it was just that I was able to quit. Still, the patterns are there: chaos, drugs, illness.

I underwent heart surgery, so my life was prolonged; my mother succumbed to her illness, and now she is gone. In terms of cycles, we both lived pretty much the same life.

So many of our parents are the carnage of the revolutionaries. Not everyone is going to be the revolutionary – the activist, the Black Panther, the power-to-the-people kind of person. I knew more about being a junkie, like my parents, than being a revolutionary – like George Jackson was. That realization made me mad for a while – until I started to put things in context. Recently I came upon some of my father's Vietnam War memorabilia. It turns out he was a war hero; I mean that's how I started to see him. Anyone who survives that horror is a hero far as I'm concerned. It made me see him differently, like the man he was – or at least was meant to be. I also learned that it was his idea to name me Maurice, which comes from the Latin word *Mauritius* meaning 'Moorish'. The Moors are from North Africa. My Dad purposefully gave me a name that showed pride in his child's Blackness, in our African ancestry. I was surprised by that. These kinds of things we learn along the way can help us see our parents better as people, and as better people. And sometimes that information can help us break destructive family cycles.

I will repeat, my parents' choices were not only on them, they were on society. Same with Eric's and his mom's. And once you can see your parents that way, victims of the world we live in, then you can love them in spite of their mistakes. That's when the forgiveness comes in. And we all need that forgiveness so we can move on and do great things, be great people. Without forgiveness, we just copy our parents, in spite of how much we hate what they did.

Deep discussion

September 5, 2011

Triny*,

Comrade's Salutation. It is fundamentally imperative that you accept this scribe in the light which governs the administration of our kind.

A mighty comrade once said, "We have surrendered all hopes of happiness for the struggle, and its' severe battles." Viewed in this context, this occurred the very moment that you and I willfully decided to engage the incumbency of enlightenment that takes the form of realism within the manly aspects of living. In this we have joined forces with our brothers and sisters who are imbibed with the highest degree of revolutionary oblation throughout the world.

I've been informed of your current displeasure with the populace that you are presently among. You must discipline your emotions brother. These particular populations that we occupy are designed so that the unconscious inmates can maliciously regurgitate our philosophical splendor. Though, not surprisingly, our way is not suited for the particular consumption of this fragment of humanity.

Your (our) peace of mind will not, and cannot, be sustained on the surface of daily interactions. Rather, it shall be stored **[ending is missing]**

* Author's comrade from Trindad.

P.S. (Press Forward)

"Convict Commoners;
our jailers grave intent to domes-
ticate our spirit or expunge us
from the earth altogether, leaves
us no choice but to plunder, in its
entirety, our righteous being into
(R)evolutionary times.

Comrades, may you all advocate of
yourself the best of health,
in mind, body, and spirit.
Be an affirmed encouragement,
through deed, and not a burden.
Make duteous expressions
that the reality of social
impoverishment,
in which we all share,
becomes a social period
which will recreate on urgency of
social balance.

In essence,
make excellent these terrible
times. For times such as these will
be as all others, inscribed in the

> books of history and in the minds and
> hearts of our seeds' future.
>
> I bid your sacrifices."

Triny is from Trinidad; he's a big man with dreadlocks but he's the gentlest soul you'll ever meet. We were in Big Sandy together, the penitentiary in Kentucky. Triny was becoming stressed and lashing out; I wanted to remind him who he was, provide him with some perspective. I wrote him a letter and handed it to him the next day I saw him. You might think because we were all in the same prison that we would see each other all the time. But it wasn't like that. It was regimented. So you passed letters when you wanted to talk to somebody about something. At least I did.

The quote in the letter was in reference to George Jackson, one of the Soledad Brothers. In 1967, Jackson wrote to his mother: "I have surrendered all hope of happiness for myself in this life to the prospect of effecting some improvement in our circumstances as a whole". That means that once you choose to struggle, you have to stop putting yourself in the category of a regular person. Regular people don't have time for the struggle because they spend their time looking for rewards. The work thing again. But some of us have learned that's not what it's all about. The reward is actually the knowledge that the struggle exists in the first place. We know that there is meaning behind the things that happen, and reasons for why life goes in certain ways. We don't expect pats on the back when we're fighting the power. The poem I wrote (the P.S.) is all about this, too; I was just thinking about my comrades, about T.

April 6, 2013

T*,

Greetings my beloved brother. May all stand well in the struggles of the manly… the universal man.

Today a prisoner, that functions with one of the white supremacy groups, got caught mixing feces into the morning breakfast grits that was being prepared for the prisoner population. When I became aware of this military plot, my first mental reaction was; what difference does it make? The kitchen workers have been preparing meals for the entire prison population, without sanitation soap, every year since I have been here. We have been devouring pure bacteria, which includes shit, for as long as I can remember.

My dear comrade, why is that people choose to probe using different atrocities as though a certain kind will determine the quality of death that is assured?

Surely, mankind has plagued itself with the very same discriminatory practices as that wicked white racist has elected to uphold.

Sincerely,
Comrade

* Author's comrade

May 28, 2013

T,

Within the ardent of respect, I humbly greet you.

I am in agreement with most of what you've written in your latest correspondence. However, I am not interested in homophobic biasness in what can be considered the traditional sense. I believe that one's sexual preference is at the pith of one's human rights, whether they are imprisoned or otherwise.

The portion of myself that may border the contoured line of homophobia was probably sowed within me at a particularly very young age. It was during an innocent period in my life with children constantly visiting and viewing people as one collective of familiar friends, all a part of the human race.

My mother, sisters, myself, and occasionally my brother, shared a house together in the projects. My mother was in a serious relationship, as it appeared, with another woman at the time. I actually loved this woman as I had witnessed my mother doing the same. One night there was a birthday party which was given to my mother. During the festivities, an argument and fight insued between this woman and my mother. Needless to say, the night of celebration was quickly ended by the actions of this woman who broke out all the windows in the house and then set it ablaze, while we were still inside of it.

This was the actual set of circumstances which caused the splitting up of my siblings and myself. Though, as traumatic as this experience was, I still however, retained an acceptance of people as kith in general, irregardless of how strange their actions may have appeared to me.

Though, the obsessive behavior that I witnessed between this woman, and my mother has left an impression on me, pertaining to these kinds of relations. Being a skeptic is quite natural considering my past experience. Also, observing with caution on the basis of the effects concerning this experience can be viewed as homophobic in some instances..

Nonetheless, I believe that much more emphasis should be placed on the impression one's behavior has on a child's mind, rather than one's biases would have on the actual behavior itself.

However, it was not tradition which my viewpoint stands on here, my dear brother, but the neglect that entered my impressionable mind, which waged my views.

We must revisit this discussion through correspondence in due course. Until then, let's continue to make manifest the betterment our understandings.

Regards,
Brother

P.S. Memo to the world: (I will Be...)

> "No one will no longer differ
> the flaws of my perfection.
> I am going to visualize it.
> Write it. Speak it.
> Try to sing and dance it. LOL.
> And if need be,
> I'll steal it,
> right from this very earth."

In the second letter, I was explaining my stance on homosexuality and where it probably originated from. I relayed the story of my mother's female partner and the drama she brought to our family when I was very young. Like I say in the letter, at one point our house was in flames, with me and my two sisters in it. All because that woman was upset with my mom. That was a scary night. My mom had to call my grandmother to come get us kids; she knew that if the fire or police department figured out what had happened, we would all get taken away from her.

In this letter I'm basically responding to what sounded like homophobia from T. It's not that I really support same-sex relationships or anything, I mean I witnessed a lot of arguing and fighting between my mother and that woman who burned our house down. Avis was her name. Having a male and female in a relationship just seems more balanced in my opinion. I was definitely angry at Avis for breaking up my family the way she did. We literally all went in different directions because of her. And ever since that incident, my mother's attitude as a mom changed. After the fire, there was not even a little bit of stability. She became nomadic – not the kind of life a kid should be leading. After a while of trying to live with her, I finally went to live with my grandmother. My sister Marquetta had already moved in with an aunt and my sister Wanda was staying with a neighbor.

I saw Avis once later on, in the neighborhood, a few years later. Lucky for her I was still a kid, too young to want revenge. I guess I was still processing. All I know is I am glad I didn't see her when I was older because I might have done something to her that I would have ended up regretting. I guess we were both lucky that way.

Anyway, what I'm explaining to T here is that, in the end, I judge people by their actions, not their identities. Lighting somebody's house on fire is a pretty evil action. But that had nothing to do with the woman being gay.

Some prison life

September 26, 2013

T,

Trust, and its' established virtues, is what shades the hearts of men who hold firm in the realm of authentic brotherhood... Homage unto you comrade.

I've wisely pondered on your viewpoint concerning the dual roles which are projected by these prison officials. My dear brother, we cannot exclude them from their good and evil displays under the guise of work and non-work distinctions. I simply argue against their unjust intrusions on the grounds that they are completely out of context. I've heard them say that, "we must see each prisoner as inhuman in order to fulfill our duties here without becoming humanly attached in some degree or another".

How does one be seen as inhuman while the general concept is suppose to be based on the implementation of rehabilitation? You also must see the irony in one particular element that is being promoted by this view. If someone, anyone, who violates a criminal statue goes to prison, somehow they are to be considered in the eyes of their officials as non-human! This is a dire problem for the prison system and, to a greater degree, for the whole of society since a mass majority of the imprisoned population will be returning back into society.

Furthermore, the officials themselves, to simply satisfy a financial portion of their lives, will need to live in a behavioral structure that requires constant re-channeling that will compromise some of the most alluring aspects of it.

My arguement shall rest here, my dear brother, but, before I make a departure, I need to present some questions. I believe that these should be placed before our offensive societal mates concerning matters that once reigned true prior to their inhuman transformation.

When our inherited poverty was persistent and the nutrients filled our bodies not... where were you? When mis-education was the only place of refuge for our starving minds... where were you? When our spirits were circumvented and we were deprived of humanity's most significant human right, the need to be loved,... where were you?

In sincerity my dear brother, allow thought to suffice...

Comrade

This third letter had to do with my opinions on prison staff and the fact that what inmates experience has nothing to do with rehabilitation. That is just the code word people use who are trying to stick up for the prison system. The fact is that a lot of those people who work in prisons don't even see inmates as human. They let us know that in all kinds of ways.

When I was at Hazelton, in West Virginia, at one point I was meeting with the Clinical Director, Dr. Gregory S. Mims. My health was really bad and all the medications and supposed care I was getting were not making things any better. I was exhausted by the constant treatments, all the measuring and analyzing and recording that went with being sick in prison. So much negotiating. I felt like giving up, so I went on strike and refused to take any more pills. What was the point? I figured I'd rather kill myself than have the prison system kill me.

That's when I got summoned to a meeting with Dr. Mims and some of the support staff who'd been attending to me. Dr. Mims told me that if I started taking my medications again he would try to get me transferred someplace that could provide better care. That seemed like a fair deal, so I cooperated. Eventually I was sent to Butner Medium II in North Carolina. It's the largest medical center of the Bureau of Prisons, so it specializes in inmates with health issues.

It's also kind of a place people go to die, like when they are at the end of life. But, as I wrote before, I knew when I got there that I would be going home. I just felt it.

Anyway, Dr. Mims and I talked a lot while I was at Hazelton. He even confided in me, telling me how hard it was to work at a place where he saw people being treated the way we were. He told me that if it wasn't so hard to kill human beings, a lot more prisoners would probably be dead. It looked like it really hurt him to witness all that went on in there. He asked me for advice, like should he stay working at Hazelton or not. I told him it looked like he didn't have much control there, what with all the federal regulations and everything, and that it was hard for him to do his job because of it. He was obviously a good man who wanted to do right. If he opened a private practice, like he was thinking, he would probably be able to benefit more people. Dr. Mims was really grateful for my perspective; he told me he thought I was sent from God. Can you believe that? There I am, an inmate, talking to this man with medical degrees. But he was a Christian who really believed we were all God's children.

Anyway, that's why I said what I said in my letter to T, how we were seen as inhuman and if it weren't for the fact that we actually *were* human, most of us would probably be dead.

```
April 11, 2014

T,

Greetings Brother...

While understanding the background for which
you, and I both stem from, it is expected
that   our   correspondence   would   venture
through the rough journey of my addiction.
And, as always, I will be straightforward
with you in exploring its blight excursion.

Being addicted served many different parts
of that larger whole in my life, especially
by me being so youthful in my mentality. Just
on the surface, there is a psychological, a
```

physical, a mimetical (peer pressure), a long with other components that magnetizes these forces that enlarges such an inharmonious condition.

It was your belief, written in your correspondence that, "if I could develop the strength which it took to stop shooting heroin so suddenly, without the help of someone, it meant that anyone has the capability to do the same." Unfortunately my friend, this belief of yours is the farthest from the truth.

Though I did not have someone's help, I did rely heavily on an ideological network. the brutal truth to kick substance abuse which I took, depended on what was the valuation of the heroin's trade in. Meaning, one's turning point of sobriety can depend on the value of something that is much more exhilarating than the actual drug itself. In reality, it is the psychological set that, what else can propel you to a comfortable stimulation in a more positive outcome, than that which had previously been engaged in a negative one. And, thereafter the greatness of individuality is efficiently sort after.

The ideological network to which I made a commitment to changing my behavior overnight was, the evolutionary obligation to Black revolution and freedom.

Defining revolution in its literal meaning as, any fundamental change or reversal of conditions. And, freedom being defined as, one who has the ability to control his or her own destiny.

Thereby, through the value of this particular ideology, it gave me an unbiased conviction not to settle for an existence that consisted of, contracting HIV/AIDS in the bowels of a frigid prison, and neglecting all sides of my manly obligations to. my family, the people, and myself.

Supreme regards my dear friend/brother….
Power to the

People.

Maurice

In this last letter to T, I wanted to clarify things around his idea that if I could stop using heroin on my own then anyone could. If that were the case, I wanted him to know, there would be a lot more rehabilitation going on in prison. But instead, most people get destroyed in there because they don't have the ideological network I have. You need a network, and I don't mean like a bunch of people to help you. Because that doesn't really exist inside. I mean that you have to reprogram yourself, come up with a new program, using yourself as the network, as the processor. You have to get to those new ideologies that you don't even know exist – or that are so spaced out from each other you can't really see them. It requires detailed studying – and thinking about things in context. I read all the time when I was in prison, even when I was high. And I wrote all the time, too, all in the name of this process. You can witness this in my letters; like, one minute I'm writing basic English sentences and the next it sounds like something out of the 1800s! That was me gathering all my ideologies together.

When I read these letters now, I see that my whole state of mind was different back then. Everything I said I believed, but I really can't imagine those thoughts now, even though they're mine. They sound out of context, poetic, and philosophical, not like me now. That's what insignificant drudge work does to a person, it takes away our philosophy. I do drudge work now on the outside but, the difference with me is that, I am still conscious. I had a chance to test the other side, the philosophical state of mind, so I know where it is in me and how to get back to it when I feel it slipping away. Consciousness can be a form of resistance. Consciousness brings opportunity – it shows it to you. I'm always looking to leave the rat race, and that's all I can do for now.

One of the books I read that really helped me understand my context in prison was *Man's Search for Meaning,* by Viktor Frankl. It got me to see that a holocaust was all around me. Most people might not think about prison that way, but once I started reading about the experience of Frankl in that concentration camp, my surroundings made some kind of sense. The Jewish Holocaust was obviously more brutal, especially physically. But psychologically, a lot of the same approaches are used in the American prison system that were used by the Nazis. Of course, once you put the word *criminal* in front of the name of someone, people don't care as much what approaches get used on them. It is much easier for most people to care about all those innocent people who were murdered in Europe during World War II than us people who committed crimes.

But some criminals can be innocent, too. Not just because we might not have done the crime we're accused of – I have already explained that I am guilty of mine – but because society took our innocence away from us way before we even got to prison. I mean, have you seen the film *13th*? How can anyone watch that and not be outraged? You have to look for meaning in everything and create an ideological network for yourself in order to not just survive but to grow, even in a dark place. That's what I did in prison. Not everyone can do that – or even wants to. That's what I was trying to tell T.

Co-author's note

Maurice is resilient. That is probably why he was able to stop using drugs, something so many prisoners never do. A 2020 *New York Times* article defines resilience as: "the ability to recover from difficult experiences and setbacks, to adapt, move forward and sometimes even experience growth". While there are several factors involved that contribute to one's resilience, research shows that genetics has little to do with it. According to one researcher of post-traumatic stress, our early relationships and how loved we felt as children, greatly inform our resilience.

Maurice's life challenges this causal argument. Although, perhaps, at a younger age than he can even recall, there were loving influences in his life. Perhaps the nurturing from his grandmother was all he needed to grow the muscles of resilience. At the same time as early security in relationships was found to be central, so was stress. We need to experience stress in order to learn how to deal with it. The article in question was written during the COVID lockdown:

> ...the tools common to resilient people are optimism (that is also realistic), a moral compass, religious or spiritual beliefs, cognitive and emotional flexibility, and social connectedness. The most resilient among us are people who generally don't dwell on the negative, who look for opportunities that might exist even in the darkest times. During a quarantine, for example, a resilient person might decide it is a good time to start a meditation practice, take an online course or learn to play guitar.
>
> Research has shown that dedication to a worthy cause or a belief in something greater than oneself — religiously or spiritually — has a resilience-enhancing effect, as does the ability to be flexible in your thinking.[1]

If placed in the context of his life in and out of prison, the above-mentioned traits are quite apparent in Maurice's thoughts and actions. Not everyone is resilient, that is what he wants to emphasize to his friend here. And people shouldn't have to be, simply to survive incarceration.

African Americans

(Behind the scene)

One particular cold and still winter night in mountainous Inez, Kentucky, my cellie and I engaged in a heated debate about Black people's need to unify. He, with piercing rebuttals, refused to acknowledge the racial context in which we now live in today, and its' institutional involvement. The discussion had gotten so death-like until I considered writing him a letter just to solicit a conscious thought from his emotional rant.

February 3, 2012

Mafuz*,

Greetings at the behest of respect. Suffice it to write ``homage", as this should be the duty of man to invoke onto man.

I accept the understanding that there exists a great possibility that this letter will not reach its' intended target with efficiency, on the basis that our Black brothers have become greatly disorganized in thought and application... Surely, it is that you are, one of these brothers.

In respect to the conversation that we engaged in the other night, let me say that when it comes to the liberation of our people, I will not fall short of delivering an in depth and factual analysis of that reality. I also, humbly apologize for not utilizing this approach the first time, given that it is also factual that conscious men do not deal in a manner that is inconclusive. From this point on, we will engage only with the facts of a topic and their alignment with the proper etiquettes.

Concerning the men of some American universities such as; Russell Conwell (Temple University), Rockefeller (co-founder, University of Chicago), John Hopkins (John Hopkins University), Cornelius Vanderbilt (Vanderbilt University), Ezra Cornell (Cornell University), James Duke (Duke University), and Leland Stanford (Stanford university): These men were called philanthropists which means; works or endeavors meant as a charitable aid or endowments intended to increase the well being of humanity. I will allot onto you a statement made by Russell Conwell (Temple University) so that you may receive an understanding of the nature of these men. The quote is from the book "A People's History of the United States" written by Howard Zinn. "I sympathize with the poor, but the number of poor who are to be sympathized with is very small. To sympathize with a man whom "God" has punished for his sins… is to do wrong… let us remember that there is not a poor person in the United States who was not made poor by his own shortcomings".

In spite of the fact that this statement is totally abhorrent, do you think that people who think in this capacity will have your best interests at heart or care about your well being? I mean that you, your family, and everyone else that you know are, according to the United States' economic structure, considered poor now, just as your ancestors were considered then.

These institutions of higher learning did not and do not encourage dissenting with this ideology. They encourage the total opposite. It is the institutions responsibility to uphold this ideology by training the middlemen ie; educators, lawyers, politicians, etc., to become loyal buffers (something that separates the entities, such as, a neutral area between two conflicting powers).

Your thoughts must become organized within the nucleus of our reality. You have stated on numerous occasions that as people of the very same ethnicity; "we do not owe each other anything". However, you became afflicted by the course of your current situation, to the point of weeping, because you feel that a system which propels these sorts of statements owes you freedoms. The system that does not favor you, owes you? But, to the people with whom you share the same affliction, you owe nothing to? Your logic is as arrogantly ignorant as Mr. Conwell's statement.

You have also stated; "all races were enslaved by their own people at some time or another", thereby passing enslavement and racism off as some coincidental happenstance. First, throughout the history of mankind, there has never been a system constructed by an African-American, that implemented slavery upon an African American. There were however, systems that needed only to be established to defend the race from many different forms of slavery.

Moreover, the continental Africans established one of the first forms of employment, which was aligned with that of servitude and not chattel enslavement, surely, a remarkable distinction. The Atlantic Slave Trade should have been coined as the Atlantic Servitude Trade, at least from the perspective of the

Africans. The concept was that we (Africans) give you (Europeans) labor in exchange for your modern technology. There are modern day forms of this systematic tradeoff being practiced today, however, the genocidal element has been excluded. Today, at the end of your duties, you can still retain the rights to your land, nation, birthrights, name, family status, and life.

There has never been any other race of people, outside of the continental Africa and the African-American race, that has experienced the catastrophic genocide associated with these races. No other race atrocities can compare in regards to the estimated number of souls that were lost in the centuries being accounted for.

Your final question was; "why should we care about the past today"? My answer would be; balance, awareness, gauge, purpose, value and guidance.

Caring about the past balances your mental, spiritual, and physical perspectives while existing in the living field of life. It makes you aware that these perspectives must be identified, defined and applied correctly on the basis of your survival in this field. It allows you to gauge, through the understanding of your inherited history, your current position within the society of your choosing. It makes your purpose in life much broader than that of self indulgence. The value of yourself becomes understood through the findings within, not without. And, it acts as a reminding mental guide *to* the essentials of your humanness, which subsequently connects you to all the rest of humanity.

My dear brother, we will build further on these things in due course, but, at this moment, I have to depart from this letter. Please be well and I'll be the same. Respects.

Sincerely,
A Friend

* Author's cell partner

Here I am writing to the man I'm sharing a cell with. Once again, I passed a letter onto a comrade. As I explained, it was sometimes the only way to communicate, to get out long thoughts and ideas. And, in this case, I desperately needed Mafuz to listen to me and he just wasn't doing that when we were talking one on one. Writing was the only way I was going to reach him because Mafuz was often aggressive and disorganized when speaking directly to people. He spoke primarily without context in his dialogue, the way so many of us have been taught to do. In our conversations, he just repeated all the lies we learned as men, as African Americans, as incarcerated people. I cared a lot about him and wanted him to really think about the things I had shared with him in our talk. The letter was my way of receiving his undivided attention.

One of the lies that really gets me is the idea that Africans and African Americans are the same, have the same experience. This shows a lack of world-consciousness. We are, socially, two separate versions of African/Black people, on the basis of where we live, our respective continents. The idea that comes from this mistaken belief, that anybody who really wants to can make it in the United States, is more of an African viewpoint than an African American one.

When Africans arrive here, in the US, that is their expectation. And that's partly because they have different experiences than African Americans do a lot of the time. Most African Americans know the context of this country, and so they don't buy into the story of what I recently learned is called *meritocracy*. We know better than to think it's all up to us.

Unfortunately, because Mafuz refuses to investigate certain ways of thinking, or ways of life that aren't like his own, he chose not to rebut me or respond. So that dialogue ended with my letter.

Co-author's note

The quote that Maurice uses in this letter from Conwell was from one of his most famous speeches, which he delivered thousands of times, mostly during the 1890s. Conwell was a former minister and helped found Temple University, as Maurice notes. This quote came from a lecture called "Acres of Diamonds" and ironically made Conwell very rich through speaking fees. By the time of his death in 1925, this speech had reportedly earned him some $8 million.

The section of the speech within which the referenced quote appears reads as follows:

> Some men say, "Don't you sympathize with the poor people?" Of course I do, or else I would not have been lecturing these years. I won't give in but what I sympathize with the poor, but the number of poor who are to be sympathized with is very small. To sympathize with a man whom God has punished for his sins, thus to help him when God would still continue a just punishment, is to do wrong, no doubt about it, and we do that more than we help those who are deserving. While we should sympathize with God's poor—that is, those who cannot help themselves—let us remember there is not a poor person in the United States who was not made poor by his own shortcomings, or by the shortcomings of some one else. It is all wrong to be poor, anyhow. Let us give in to that argument and pass that to one side.[2]

This references a larger issue that remains on Maurice's mind: that myth that everyone can pull themselves up by their bootstraps. This is the simplified version of Booker T. Washington's theory of productivity that Maurice felt his cousin Eric had inherited from his mother. As he regularly points out, not just *anyone* can do *anything* – and that's because of the obstacles that tend to hinder some more than others. Those obstacles are typically outside the control or responsibility of the individual in question.

Philosophies and practice

April 2, 2013

Maaj*,

Homage Sensei.

In reference to the question that you posed before me recently, I find it very simple, yet protracted, in nature. When one engages in a refined observation within their very own self, even though these may have been great attempts to obtain a simple answer, it is, perhaps, much more complex than the fundamentals of thought can actually convey.

"Who Are You?". Its' summoned request can stifle the best of men. And, its' answer can elude even the most in depth thinkers of any dapper ethnicity.

Knowing that you have accepted the energy of my natural sincerity and have a better understanding of my ideology than most, I can expound that the answer soundly reverts back to a predetermined question. I can only suggest who I am by first having some degree of understanding of what I am in our species, as well as, the ability of our particular species. The first word which comes to mind, that is capable of a definition, is "Evolutionist". Through this respective analogy, I can be many things. I can be transformed into anything within the species faculty, during different periods thoughout the course of my living.

There are moments within a period when I am a reflection of a confused adolescent minded man-child, searching for a balanced equilibrium that will define the meaning of human purpose. Then, there are those moments, within a period, where my mind transforms into a mega organism that perpetuates the idea that I am a compliment of everything atomic that lies in the entirety of the cosmos. This urbane thought process equates me to that of a supreme Creator and falls within the working scheme of universal order.

I find the elusiveness of your question quite intriguing...

Honors,
Pupil

* Author's mentor

June 4, 2013

Maaj,

Within respect, I greet you, trusted advisor.

To my surprise sir, it was the downpour of a rainy day which sparked those partisan thoughts of mine. The ravings of one who is imposing upon unambiguous freedom is the insignia of royalty to which humans are inclined. Regardless of the circumstances, whether self-inflicted or externally applied, we all desire freedom in its' elixir form… do we agree?

Long before my incarceration, my vision of society and of the world had been obstructed. I simply could not see either of them as I wanted or needed to. Without regret, I make reference here that this lack of visions and their subsequent events that followed, such as incarceration, are both very evil experiences. You yearn so much to be free during these circumstances, which seem never to cave, that your spirit begins to descend into a prolonged captivity of iniquity. It becomes the stilts which provide a vehicle for human struggle.

Stumbling about and trying to right these wrongs with wrong is a guarantee for a visionless and incomprehensible youth. Freedom from the circumstances of blindness and incarceration. Freedom from the suffering perpetuated by these circumstances. Freedom from the consequences which both entail. This is the cycle that addresses the human soul each and every second of your life.

```
May the Universal Creator favor you and
yours, to the extreme in prosperity leader...
```
Supreme Regards,
Pupil

Noah self-proclaimed the name, Maaj, at some point. He was evolving and felt his name should evolve, too. He went back and forth between different names, and I found myself addressing him differently, depending on mood. His and mine. We met in prison. Noah was ten years younger than I was, but he was a mentor – and a friend. Age doesn't matter; certain people are here to guide us, and they can look all kinds of ways and come from all kinds of places. Noah was the first younger man that I felt could have been an oracle; I never met anybody with that much wisdom. He really made me stop my whole life and question everything I was taught. Everything someone sees in me now pretty much started with him.

Maaj literally asked me to consider the question, "who are you?". I enjoyed these opportunities to let my mind run away from my body, to imagine and philosophize. That was something I could do with Maaj. He made me talk! I just came up with the word, 'Evolutionist', because it was a good description of life. It was a description of me. Later, I referenced (r)evolutionist, like George Jackson did in his letters. That was taking it a step further.

To me, an Evolutionist is about making progress, about accepting that things are progressing if they're not how you want at the time. The question is, are you willing to deal with what you're evolving into? I was an Evolutionist – I saw myself as this. As

I think about it now, this is probably the cause of the problems in my life – even now. I am an innovator, which for some people has a bad connotation. It means the opposite of tradition, of comfort, of staying in the same place. Evolutionists and Traditionalists don't usually get along.

August 20, 2013

Noah*,

Homage, my friend.

Of course, I do have much to add when it comes to the transsitional process from my mental boyhood to my mental manhood. I will express these dues diligently, as the character of my spirit strives to do. It is that I have worked tirelessly to try and master my manhood.

Transition is always needed to benefit progress while change is the chemistry of nature itself. Nothing remains the same through the seasons. Even life and death repeat the same cycle, each evolving in a repetitive process that is uniquely different.

A boy must make this transition in an evolving cycle that is unique to his own individuality. It will be the course of his liberation. By learning who we are as an individual, within the midst of billions, we begin to know ourselves.

Everyday our lives should, and must, be spent in a climb to surmount the great mountainous height that is manhood. Therefore, my friend, let this be the hallmark of axioms which establish the obtainment of manhood.

I look forward in connecting with you very soon...

Supreme Regards,
Tyree

* Author's prison friend

August 23, 2013

Maaj,

Peace Sir. As the presence of peace is cultivated first within one's mind state.

Today, at the conclusion of my meditation session, I became overwhelmed at being centered in the knowledge that I, myself, have engaged in acts of deception against my ancestors and their sacrifices. My family, their struggles. My race, their needs. My comrades, their misery. My cause, its' precision. My freedom, its' necessity. Myself, and its' mastery.

As the truly faithful (r)evolutionary must consider deceit upon his very own lot, an act of treason.

```
These energies must immediately be placed
in their appropriate perspectives.

                                    Respects,
                                    Student
```

When I talk about a meditation session in prison, you have to understand that with all the chaos going on around, it's not like the meditation some people might imagine. It would resemble more like a football player in the fourth quarter of a playoff game. It's that same kind of excessive focus in the moment. Athletes, military personnel, prisoners... These meditation sessions of mine would sort of come on, instead of me choosing to take some specific time to meditate. I might be in the middle of a workout and just have to stop and hold the thoughts that were pouring in. I grieved this way, too. All of a sudden, right in the middle of something, I might think about my grandma dying, and just start crying.

I didn't feel I had control over the direction of my feelings very much. I would go into my cell and just let it all out. I might take five or ten minutes, then wipe my face clean and go do what I had to do. Writing these letters was another form of meditation. I really never decided to meditate, as much as meditation decided it was time. I once took a class with a Hindi yogi in prison, and he gave us some insight into the practice. For one thing, he saw the original idea of meditation being commercialized. I mean you're not going to see people all over India in the Lotus position. It's so much bigger than that. As I did more reading, I learned that meditation was really about nothingness. When you meditate, you try to strip yourself of excess. If you're focusing on taking some specific position with your body, that can't be nothing-ness.

As for the treasonous acts I mention in the last letter, I go into this more in my "Letter of Resignation" – the Epilogue to this book. So there will be more about all that.

```
October 2, 2013

Noah,

All due respects on the input for T.O.R.A.*.
This thing must be rooted in an absolute
morale for the excluded inhabitants in
the world. Man, that capitalism thing has
overwhelmed the souls of the population. I
do agree that the word rebel, especially as
it relates to most European societies, has
an aqqressive impingement to it.

Though, from the prospective of the conscious
ghetto Black, it becomes an inevitable
process and therefore, I am a rebel by force
and not by choice.

Slavery was forced on me… I rebel. A foreiqn
land was forced on me… I rebel. My history
was hidden from me… I rebel. An ideology of
education, lanquaqe, and religion was forced
on me… I rebel. I rebel and will always
rebel until I'm reunited with myself. It is
for this reason that I offend this country
for defending my misplacement within it.
```

```
Thanks again. Great things lie ahead of us,
my friend...

                              Until Next Time,
                                       Maurice

* The Orphaned Rebel Artistry, a non-profit
organization
```

I was inspired by Noah, but I think I inspired him a little, too. Like he was excited when I came up with this idea to start a group in prison called The Orphaned Rebel Artistry. My thinking was that most of us were orphans in one way or another, and that could be a good starting place for connections. From my ancestry as a kidnapped African, to being shipped off to my grandmother's house when mom couldn't take care of me anymore, I saw myself as coming from a long line of children without parents. That's a common bond in prison, and on the streets. Unfortunately, the group never got off the ground.

Witness

```
October 7, 2013

Noah,

Respect, my good friend...

This week has seen several incidents that
have ignited the deployment of some in
depth psychological strain. There was one
incident in particular, however, which more
effectively protruded ahead of the others.
The other day, this white guy in my unit
```

finally reached the zenith of his discontented condition.

I was taking a shower and while I was doing so, in an adjacent stall, a fellow prisoner committed suicide, apparently by hanging himself. It's during times like these that your emotions surface from that unknown place in your mind where they have been held captive. It's a foreign feeling and its' re-appearance rattles you mightily. It is also during these times that the cement barrier, that colonizes us on account of our race, comes tumbling down and the essence of character which illuminates a human being is exposed.

I actually had the honor of being formally introduced, through meaningful conversation, with this man several weeks before his death. Though, he possessed an unique personality (like that of a derisive comedian), what stood out the most was the impressive and general advocacy of libertarianism. He was insightful, intelligent, and very in tune with the dynamics of our present environment.

In the aftermath of this incident the only support that was lent by the administration was to the correctional officer who found the corpse. I have absolutely no quarrels with prison officials lending support to an officer who has experienced such an unfortunate act but, at the same time, I feel that this supportive gesture must extend beyond the comraderie of the staff. I think that immediately after a loss within the realm of the prisoner population there should also be a supportive appendage offered to his fellow prisoners. This is not simply because it's the human thing to do, but also because it can prevent these emotions that are largely unknown, from dissolving back into the captivity that occurs when they are replaced, as they always are, by the unfavorable race relations of the prison.

You comprehend these particular circumstances quite well my friend. That is to say, the prisoner's wretched psychological state. Surely, if something isn't done to re-orient the prisoners mind set, because the practical rehabilitation propriety remains theoretical, then these types of unfortunate acts will persist, inside and outside of prison.

I beseech the Creator's creative forces to favor you and all which you uphold in the implementation of righteousness.

Supreme Regards,
Maurice

I mentioned a suicide I witnessed in this letter. That day was tough. They were doing the count – counting the prisoners – during the time some of us were taking showers. That's when they discovered the guy. He had hung himself from the shower head. The guard tried to get him down but instead just kept making it worse, the way the man had attached himself and all. There was a lot of yelling. Guards were crying. But that man was not going to be stopped. You could tell by the way he situated himself, so he couldn't get back to standing even if he wanted to. I remember thinking how young the guy was. Once they finally got the body down, the staff tried to act like they were attempting to bring him back to life. But he was dead. Everybody knew that.

It's funny, because a few weeks before, I spoke to the guy for the first time. He seemed to me kind of like Rodney Dangerfield – making light of stuff, but still serious at the same time. He was in the library a lot, like I was. He was planning out his case. He told me the day I spoke to him, "I'm outta here". What I started to learn was that white guys saw suicide as better than dying in prison. I had one literally say to me: "I would rather kill myself than die shitting on myself in prison". It wasn't so much macho, it sounded more spiritual when they said it. I think maybe it's because white men aren't as used to living in the manure the way so many of us Black men are. That said, I was at that point at least once, thinking death would be better than remaining in that prison and taking their medications for the rest of my life. I was feeling like a hostage, a slave. And I guess I did not see the justification in being made to feel that way, even if I *was* a Black man.

My sister, Marquetta, she killed herself by hanging, too, about a year after I got out of prison. It was strange, but when I finally went to her house after, I noticed a whole bunch of photos were missing – the ones in frames that usually covered the coffee table in the living room. Generations of our family had been displayed there, including photographs of me. But that day there were only two photos, one at each end of the table. One was of Marquetta's grandmother, my mother's mom. I never met her, but she and Marquetta had a close relationship for a while. The other photo was of our mother. I think my sister just wanted to go see them, like she was chasing what she believed was on the other side of this life, chasing love. Maybe that's what all these prisoners who kill themselves are chasing, too – love. Because it wasn't going to be found in prison.

Co-author's note

Suicide is the leading cause of death in jail, and has only recently been given attention equivalent to its gravity. According to a 2016 piece by *The Marshall Project*, prison suicides have increased dramatically since 2001. In 2014, suicides represented 7% of all deaths in state and federal prisons. Racially, suicides are the cause of death for 7% of white prison inmates, as compared to 3.5% of Black prisoners. This is an interesting statistic to consider alongside the experience Maurice had of white men threatening suicide more often than his Black peers.

"This [racial differential] mirrors the overall increase of suicide among white men between the ages of 45 and 64 in the general population", according to the Centers for Disease Control and Prevention. Just like those on the outside, many inmates live with mental health challenges. But these issues tend to be magnified once incarcerated, such that learning about the loss of a loved one, being sent to solitary, experiencing the all too commonplace violence of prison, or being denied parole, can set someone over the edge.

Research also shows conclusively that the high rate of suicide can be traced back to the dire lack of mental health care for incarcerated people – something that Maurice emphasizes throughout this book and hopes to contribute to changing. *The Marshall Project* interviewed Dr. Michele Deitch, from the School of Law at the University of Texas, in Austin. She argues that one of the best ways, statistically, to get prisons to improve their attention to mental health care is to sue facilities for negligence in that area. There is typically a marked change towards improvement in attention and treatment with regard to suicide prevention after such legal action, according to Deitch.[3]

However, legal action is not always adequate motivation for a prison system. For example, a 2019 study by the *San Francisco Chronicle* found that even though California's penal system was "under federal court order to remedy its 'systemic failure… to deliver necessary care to mentally ill inmates' since 1995", adequate mental health care was still rarely provided. In the court's decision, Justice Anthony Kennedy wrote: "Prisoners in California with serious mental illness do not receive minimal, adequate care" and that "because of a shortage of treatment beds, suicidal inmates may be held for prolonged periods in telephone-booth sized cages without toilets".

A pattern of disinterest in prisoners with suicidal ideation was rampant. An audit of California prisons found that prison staff regularly failed to perform requisite checks on vulnerable prisoners, provide appropriate cells, or transport prisoners to medical staff in a timely manner. San Quentin State prisoner, George "Mesro" Coles-El, was quoted as saying: "Their idea of suicide watch is to wrap you in a mattress suit and put you in a cell by yourself until you don't have these feelings anymore. I don't feel like that's a very effective way to treat someone who feels like their life should end prematurely".[4]

One initiative at the forefront of prison reform is the reduction – or complete eradication – of isolation. Prisoners in isolation often attempt or succeed in killing themselves. And, at the least, they are often traumatized by the experience and then receive no subsequent counseling. Perhaps reading this book will bring to light just how desperate the situation is in American prisons, such that human lives are being lost daily for no other reason than there seems no other way out to so many prisoners. This certainly does not lay the groundwork for rehabilitation, when those allegedly intended for rehabilitation are dead.

October 16, 2013

Noah,

Greetings my good friend...

You suggested that racism is one of the key elements behind the African-American's massive incarceration woes. The truth is that racism absolutely does exist, on a great scale, in both our main society as well as in prison society which is also where the philosophy that is imbued in the criminal justice system regarding its' duties relative to crime and punishment can be found. The numbers contained in various social statistics verify this truth.

I have witnessed racism's methodical and elusive flutter in levels of manners, each and every day I've spent behind these prison walls. I am assured of this by the counterfeit personalities displayed daily by both Black and White, ranked and un-ranked officials. My empirical insight is unmistakedly reflected in the clear and certain actions of the White officers while in the Black officers they are revealed in a spectacle of behavioral uncertainty. A phenomenal display of prejudicial superiority dictates every quantum of this environment.

Nonetheless, for us Black prisoners it is well understood that neither of the officers hold any obligation in their human duties to us. Upon crossing the threshold of the prison their societal identity is tucked away and the lucidity of this reveals that today's racism is not the same as the old one. It has become remarkably evolved. The only thing that it lacks is a need to be redefined.

However, racism may not absolutely be one of the key elements to the African-American's mass incarceration woes. There is another that exceeds racism by far. That element, which we must rid our-selves of, is the notion that one particular party is displaying the role of being a human being (officials), while the other (prisoners), are displaying the role of being inhuman. When placed into a specific perspective that is obviously human, then it can be seen that one role involves simply being a violator of a specific law (human behavioral law). And the inhuman woes will be appropriately addressed in respects to the crime and in the stability of the punishment.

Farewell,
Maurice

In my October 16th letter to Noah, I was talking about race. It's hard to explain but race is a level thing in prison. Like the first level order is "us against them" – guards versus prisoners. But then after that, it becomes situational. Like this one time, I had just gotten out of the prison hospital after my bypass. I mean my chest had been broken into, the scars were fresh. But the cops were harassing me anyway, like they do (we use the words *cops* and *guards* the same by the way – and *cops* is a nice word for some of these men). Anyway, some of my Black brothers tried to step in for me and, of course, they got assaulted, too. It was one of those moments where the brothers were just tired of it all, so things got heated.

The guards called for reinforcements, until there were about 20 of us and 20 of them. And I was right in there, with my makeshift knife-proof vest on – to protect my newly operated chest. The cops told me to go to my cell, but I didn't. I learned early on it's better to stay with the group for whatever's about to happen than to isolate yourself and become an easy target for some deranged cop. I was trying to prevent an even worse whipping than what was about to be coming to all of us at that moment. Then, all of a sudden, the leader of the white prisoners stands up and says: "We're with the Blacks". Now the guards were outnumbered, so they gave up. Just for that moment. Like I said, things are situational. This is one of the lessons I learned in the classroom that's prison.

Everything we do in life can be considered school. School is school, but so is growing up in a rough neighborhood, selling drugs, and going to prison. I have chosen to learn from all my schooling, and I keep on learning now that I'm out. What I learn, I like to pass on to others, maybe save them a couple years or so. And my brothers do the same for me. I have learned all manner of things in these life classrooms. It's all about exchanging information and ideas – that's how we grow and learn. That's how we create community. That's human connection.

```
November 17, 2013

Maaj,

Supreme  respects  sir...  I deploy  my  gracious
energy   with   an   overwhelming   projection
of peace.
```

A re-orientation of my thoughts shall be the highest of priorities in these few days that are ahead of me. My thoughts, and events in recent days, were not, in most ways, accepting of one another. There have been some forces outside of myself that are making attempts at distracting my attention. Fortunately, I am in no position to allow my mind to submit to impaired thinking.

I'm going to take an analytical attitude towards this by analyzing some of the most intimate details of my thinking and determine their efficiency in making situations manifest.

The constancy of my mental state has been causing much agony to the state of my physical well being. In essence, every thought which protrudes from my mind is ultimately taxing upon the entirety of myself. Some people say that this is a process which one encounters when he, or she, is entering into a form of transformation or an awakening. What is exceptionally peculiar about the timing of this encounter is that I feel like I am being awakened in an environment that seems to be designed to accommodate a person who is mentally dead.

I must solemnly admit that, at this moment, I am bewildered. It feels strange that I am placing this burden of mine before you as I fully know that, in the end, it is only myself who can aid and assist in my thoughts.

Because I have allowed my mind to become akin to frustration, I am familiar with the reasoning that there is, surely, no refuge from the presence of one's own bothersome mind.

I disembark in respect,
Pupil

I can't remember specifically what was bothering me here. I am pretty sure it was something dealing with prison and not home or personal issues. A constant emotional issue for me in prison was the way I was up against so many of my brothers when it came to discussing mental and spiritual health. The hardest fights I fought were with my religious counterparts who were so deeply convicted about their religious beliefs, but not conscious at all. My ideology, I really believe, helped me free myself mentally – and maybe even physically – from prison. I felt I could see things that they couldn't, and I wanted to spend time in enlightening discussions, talking about things inside and outside our set belief systems. But, instead, I spent a lot of time just plain arguing with men and ending up looking like some weirdo because I was not dealing in "tradition", as seen by the others. Like I said in the letters, I felt like I was being awakened in an environment that seemed designed to accommodate only people who were mentally dead. It was a lonely existence a lot of the time.

December 3, 2013

Noah,

Albert Einstein once stated; "there are a fine percentage of children who are born geniuses, but the vast majority of them begin to be degeniunized from the moment that they come into contact with their parent's way of life".

I have no data before me that refutes, or proves true, Mr. Einstein's statement. I will imply, however, based on personal experience and observation, that as our children are born into our lives, we seldom consider at that time and as parents, whether they have any skillful or talented possibilities until, maybe, they reach their adolescent years, if we consider it at all.

I, myself, was born into what I've coined; "A Black Peasant's Woe". This is in reference to an African-American from the lowest class of society being born into a chaotic and dysfunctional way of life. These particular woes have, however, imbued in myself an intolerable state of mind regarding the suffering of children that are entwined in circumstances and geographical locations similar to my own experience.

I can almost vividly remember, back in the seventies following my birth in 1973, when my mother and others within and surrounding my household use to, quite often, highlight my unyielding interest in many things. Then, rather suddenly when I was around four or five years of age, it appeared that the atmosphere in our two bedroom apartment changed for the worse. My mother began to physically abuse my two sisters, my brother and myself on, what felt like, every single day of the week and month during those confusing years. I barely survived the attacks which ranged from attempted drownings to my collarbone being fractured on one occasion.

There were only a couple of ways that I would be able to escape these brutal attacks. The heroic pleas offered by my eldest sister to fend off my mother or, when I knew that she was due home from work, I would afflict myself with some kind of childish injury, usually a bloody nose, so that she would not impose any further injury on my person.

In the aftermath of these things and most likely because of them, I have developed a severe inability to focus on my talents, skills, or adolescent remnants. After these events, as I was growing up, I spent my energies acting out and mentally, and physically, preparing for the danger that I envisioned was going to be inevitable. This method of survival has carried deep into my adulthood and although, many attempts are being made to train these things out of myself, there still yet remains some traces of its' existence.

It's hard to wonder sometimes if it was fortunate or unfortunate that I could not comprehend the effects of heroin, cocaine, and alcohol. Its' usage by my mother, father, and their friends turned them into unrecognizable zombies. So, was it fortunate, as I had no idea as to what was turning these people against me and themselves. Or, was this an unfortunate lack of understanding which placed me at a disadvantage in trying to help my family overcome these misfortunes.

Currently, it is impossible for me to fathom a spiritual, mental, or physical assault waged on the well being of any child. No matter what their biological origin, race, creed, or ethnic background, the growth and development of all children must be protected. Whether they're an Afgan refugee, a child soldier in Sierra Leone, or living in the ghetto neighborhoods of North America, I wholly have no tolerance for their suffering. I also suggest here that anyone who does not share my concern and temperament in this matter should be expunged from this planet called Earth.

I conclude, my friend, that I will still, however, wrestle with certain psychotic responses in some areas of my life because of my past ordeals. I hold no ill will towards my mother, father, or their friends for the roles they played in this. They are all intriguing people who were also caught up in a condition of depressive woes. This condition has seduced the mightiest of people, turning their beautiful morale inside out.

Though the statement that was made by Mr. Einstein cannot be proven through any scientific analysis that I am personally aware of, this does not change the fact that we must not ignore our enormous responsibility to protect our children, even from the imperfection of ourselves. In these present days, we may employ the most sophisticated rationale as to why the world is in the state that it is in, but, we never equate our contributions to this state of woe.

Thank you again my friend for your attention in allowing me to express a viewpoint on this particular subject.

Sincerely,
Maurice

Co-author's note

Research shows unequivocally that childhood abuse and neglect are a part of most every incarcerated person's background. Using the Adverse Childhood Experience (ACE) measurement, studies show that while around 61% of the general population have suffered some kind of traumatic childhood experiences, that close to 97% of incarcerated persons have undergone similar experiences. ACEs are also linked to physical health issues, in the short and long run, something that Maurice continues to wrestle with even today. But, as a 2022 article from the Urban Institute argues: "when criminal legal system leaders develop crime reduction strategies, they often focus only on deterring crime or appealing to rational choice". Instead, they argue, in order to truly address the core issues of criminality, those in charge of the U.S. penal system should be supporting the systematic inclusion of "trauma-informed resources".[5]

This is a foundational theme in Maurice's writings, that mental health issues are left by the wayside once a person steps inside a prison. And because of this, he believes violence, despair, and recidivism become the norm for the incarcerated – even after they are released.

What is laid out in this particular letter by Maurice is a heartbreaking story of a childhood filled with chaos and violence. The fact that there seemed to be a time early on in Maurice's life where he received actual encouragement, makes his future childhood all the more painful to read. There had apparently been a moment when some family members were actually capable of nurturing children. But clearly that ended abruptly, and what came next was the kind of abuse that stays in a person's body for the rest of their life.

At first, as is common, Maurice turned to drugs, emulating his parents' choices. And then that became his business – maybe one of the few things in which he was seen as successful. His skills suited that line of work. After a while, his life led him to violence which led him to prison. It looked like just one more downhill spiral of a Black man raised in a household struggling financially and emotionally, in a country that continues to overlook its systemic problems.

But, for him, his childhood experiences had also produced empathy, such that he cannot *tolerate* the *suffering* of a child. Maurice was later able to find the ability to mentally process through his own writing, and intentionally sought out people in whom he could confide. And he has forgiven his parents, as well. All of these components are necessary for healing, according to most mental health professionals. But all of this forging ahead is not typical for those who have been abused, neglected, and placed into a prison cell. Just imagine if there was attention paid to mental health and healing as soon as a person entered the prison system. But, instead, prison administrators talk of aspirational possibilities and blame the deficit of care on insufficient funding. Maurice forged ahead on his own, but that is not something most people are capable of – whether inside or outside of prison.

Black dreams

September 4, 2014

Maaj,

I often ask the brothers who live in the intensified life of an underclassman, what is the end game? Is it a lifespan of chaotic episodes? A constant state of inferiority through practical karma, by the implementation of the crab-in-the-bucket syndrome? Or, were we born as some of those insects which seem to only exist to be eaten by other larger, or more wiser invertebrates? I most times can't twist my mind around other people's reason for being. This being a peculiar existence may perhaps be an understatement. While other cultures seek a massive amount of power, we simply seek to be empowered to feel human. Think about this for a moment brother. Needing to be empowered, to feel natural, or fit into our natural way of creation, our birthright in its essence!

I will share an ancient dream of mine with you, my friend. In the final phase of my life, I will live somewhere in the remotest region of a continent, amongst an indigenous tribe (preferably Africa or India). I will take on a wife that is the most obvious in thought and appearance. I would join her in rearing as many beautiful children as our ages will allow. The mornings will find me toiling the earth, planting and harvesting all that my family will need of the earth to survive. My evenings will be spent conveying to my wife and children all that I see which reign beautiful in them, and within the atmosphere of this precious universe. And, I will enjoy the confinement of the night while thrusting sensually and deeply between the thighs of my wife, as if I was encountering the pleasure of her hymen for the very first time.

My dear brother, in this I will only seek the basis elements of living as should be the design of every nation, unto every man.

Until we connect again, I ask that the universal Creator favor your intentions. Please be well.

Maurice

In this letter, the "we" I am talking about is Black people. And when I write that I "can't twist my mind around other people's reason for being", I am attempting to ask why other Black people don't see what I see. Of course, Noah – aka Maaj – always knew exactly what I was saying. He was an exception. That's how come I could share my dream with him. But like I have said before, I often felt (and feel) like a weirdo, an outcast, even with my "own" people.

That dream I wrote about is actually in progress in my life right now. Some of it can't be anymore, obviously, like having young children. But I do have grandchildren.

This grand vision is a part of my aim, my goal every single day. I tell my wife, Kim, all the time that I want a country life, that I yearn for that. The city is a trigger for me now and I can feel it taking a toll on my mental health on a daily basis. I am always on a high state of alert; that's what the city does to me. It's habit. Once I had the sharpness of mind to thrive in the street, now I'm just a nervous wreck. Like an old football player I recall all the plays, but I could not execute them even if I tried. And my body remembers all the injuries, too, and still has that self-defense mechanism in place. It's like I am on the field/in the streets even though I'm not anymore.

So I walk around on ready-set. I mean, I'm even scared of the dark now. If it isn't daytime, then I'm not hanging with my friends. I tell them I can meet in the daylight but, come nighttime, I need to be home, behind my locked doors. I have seen enough people go back to the streets when they have no business doing so. Like when an athlete who should have retired just wants one more big game – or paycheck – these guys I know go out there and get eaten. That life requires absolute commitment and focus, and that's just not something you can still have at a certain point in your life. They end up back in jail, or dead. So, yes, I need to retreat to the country as soon as I possibly can. It's kind of an emergency.

Studies

October 24, 2013

Professor K*,

It is impossible for me not to be attracted to the characteristics of the Inside-Out Prison Exchange Program, whether or not I'm in agreement with its' philosophy. The fact is that its' theoretical knowledge, shared practical experiences concerning imprisonment; and the prisoner's re-entry back into mainstream society are elements which are a vested part of my past, present, and future. Whether taken in the context of my family's well being or in the progression/regression of my peer culture, the promise of investment offered engulfs my life.

This new assignment, the Social Disorganization Theory, stands in my thoughts as a paradox. It has an incongruous quality in the way that it is applied here. I challenge this as a theory in the form of a letter as I feel that the forum of classroom sessions would be considered inappropriate for such a contest.

Sociologists who endorse this particular theory suggest that: If you were to remove an established ethnic group from its' environment and replace them with another, completely different ethnic group, would the latter groups condition remain the same as the former group's if the environmental living structure was the same. Of course, this study is aimed at pinpointing whether there are problems with the actual structure of the environment, or a problem with the actual ethnic group's disposition.

I've studied, sincerely and tediously, on these kinds of matters and it has become clear to me that while the sociologists have a well intended theory of "Social Disorganization", it is not, in any sense, just theoretical. It has been practiced throughout history, globally across societies, and in many different forms. Furthermore, it is still being utilized in this very day and age.

Keep in mind that the concept of disorganization is not simply designated in the form of physicality. It can also be assigned to the mental replacement of a mass group of people as well.

The undertaking of replacing an ethnic group's thought processes with that of another is a common practice, especially during times of great strife in a society. It is a classic way to avoid a rebellion. Please allow and gear your research towards the end of the African Slave Trade and the middle and end of the American Civil War. The Americas then were still thought of as the New World and the maintaining of one thought, one law, and one goal was needed. It was this vital need which kept the new, so called free slaves, and poor Whites cooperating peacefully with the elite and self proclaimed governments during those times.

When a particular ethnic group, in any society, begins to perpetuate signs of educational and professional decline, shares an enmity towards balancing economic imbalances, and no longer shows an acceptance of the status quo's normalcy as it's normalcy then it is engaging in a variation of rebellion. As a result, this can cause the group to be labeled as a societal offender, or be at risk of mental rehabilitation or physical replacement.

Where it concerns the United States of America, the structure that perpetuates the status quo has been solidly established and will be enforced, as it always has, in accordance with history. The results are still practical. Every generation of every ethnic group in the U.S., in any environment within its' borders will, unless it engages in any form of persistent protest, submit to, in their own unique custom, to the established structure. If they don't they risk being subjected to rehabilitation or replacement by the government of the United States of America.

Upon your request, we can elaborate at great length about this analogy and the remainder of the assignment's theories (labeling, strain, etc.), which were informatively presented during class.

Respectfully,
Maurice

*Sociologist facilitating The Prison Exchange Program from the local university

These next few letters are to Dr. Jeri Kirby, a professor at West Virginia University. She was the Bureau of Prisons Federal Coordinator of the Inside-Out Prison Exchange Program, which the class I was in was a part of. She is a professor of Criminal Justice – and an ex-convict, too. She did some time at a low-security prison. The course was nine months long.

These letters were journal assignments for class. We were told we could write in any form we wanted, and I had discovered by then that letters helped me think and process. We were supposed to share any and all personal feelings and thoughts. Nothing was off-limits. The class itself was basically a practical and theoretical understanding of incarceration. The theoretical aspect came with the college students who were studying alongside us in prison; they came to the prison every week.

There were fifteen criminology students and fifteen incarcerated students. We were hand-picked, you couldn't just sign up for the class. At this high security prison, security was the big issue. Those who were chosen to attend the class were the leaders of various prison groups. I felt I had been conditioned and prepared to do a class like this. It would have been too exhausting for some people's brains – truthfully most of the guys just couldn't hang with something like this. But a few of us were already doing it, both looking around *and* within ourselves. So the program was like an add-on, an outside perspective of what we had been doing for a while on our own. We were ready.

This was also a really difficult time for me, and I was in a certain kind of place when I wrote this stuff. I delved into a lot during and after that program. But, like I said before, some of those thoughts I had then are not my thoughts now. Anyway, I had no problem with basically being studied in that class. *Use me, dissect me*, I thought. That was my mission – and still is – to have people understand me and the other human beings imprisoned by the system. I have no problem with people studying me if it leads to a better understanding of the conditions inside.

This makes me think of Aaron Hernandez, the football player who killed himself in prison. He donated his brain to science and, when they studied it, they found he was suffering from the same disease that other football players had. Doctors finally accepted that all of those concussions added up and affected players' mental health. That helped people to understand why Hernandez did what he did – and other football players, too. I hope this all leads to doctors treating these athletes better, just like I want prisoners to get treated better – all of us, more like humans.

Me and my comrades went into that class wanting to be used, like I said. But soon it seemed like the college students were the lab rats and the prisoners were the scholars. The students had such a superficial understanding of the life we were leading, but after a while they started seeing that it was a systemic problem they were looking at. Human beings were being tortured; there was more to the story than they read in their textbooks. I remember one of the students asking us: "Why do I have access to all this information out there – books, the internet… but you know more than I do?" Let's just say we had a lot of time to think about the situation, to observe things from the inside, so to speak.

The students were from all walks of life. There was this one young woman who reminded me of a Barbie doll. She seemed *real* privileged. Well, by the end of the class, she was the most distraught of everyone. She just could not believe what was happening in the prison. She couldn't even get through her speech at our graduation ceremony. (We actually had to have two graduations, like a pre-graduation ceremony before the more public one. Once the administrators saw how emotionally charged and connected we all were, how much everyone had changed and grown, they got nervous. The bureaucrats didn't want to risk too much honest talk about the horrors of prison and what needed changing. They just hadn't anticipated the realness that would happen).

I tried to participate in another Inside-Out class once I got out. It was online, through Arcadia University in Pennsylvania. It was not as meaningful. I still was one of the "inside" students because I had been incarcerated, but being out I didn't have that same sort of raw rage or the honesty that comes from being locked up. Pushing all the stories and feelings out was harder on the outside because I wasn't yearning for the same kind of release anymore. Plus, being on Zoom did not work for me. I mean, they were asking me to go deep, yet half of them wouldn't even turn on their cameras to show their faces. It didn't feel authentic.

```
November 13, 2013

Professor K,

This week's class assembly probed a proposed
question; What are your thoughts on the
current state of recidivism and re-entry?

Here again, I'm submitting a personal summary
via a journal, for the sake of respectfully
preserving, in light of my personal views,
the proper etiquettes of the assembly forum.

First, the answer can only start with
the indoctrination of rehabilitation and
the potential of its' universal methods.
The current non-system places a, soon
to be released, prisoner at an absolute
disadvantage when the resources available to
the prisoner are realistically compared to
the reality of high unemployment rates, skill
```

requirements, and the lack of acceptance by the society at large of the individual.

For these reasons and, of course, many others, it appears to not make a bit of difference as to what I may particularly think, or for that matter know, even if the facts are based on my many experiences. Any transformations, typically self induced, that better the quality of their behavior and that occur during their confinement, will only be made insubstantial or invalid *by* contradictory maxims like paying one's 'debt to society, or by lack of preparation like treadmill incarceration that are hallmarks of the criminal justice system.

I will sincerely express here that the practice of realism must be incorporated into any discussion concerning matters of today's mainstream society and its' sister, prison society.

The fact of the matter is that my arguments will be labeled as un-American for implying that our government, for decades, has allowed a steady flow of illicit drugs and weapons to cross our nation's borders with the intent to destroy both urban and suburban communities within our country. This has occurred with unmitigated impunity and is a_direct perpetuation of discord that goes to the core of recidivism and problems with re-entry.

Of course, I'll be told that I should direct my improbable energy to things other than the folly of a delusional conspiracy theory. Now, the tedious studying of the sciences of culture, government, economics, etc… are fashionable, but, they lack relevancy from the viewpoint of a prisoner. Adding to this is the President's decision to activate yet another multi-million dollar prison instead of building a multimillion dollar vocational facility that is more in line with recent crime rates, which are level or down in most areas. This is a clear sign of what is truly intended by government for the citizens of its' society.

To the marginal thinker it will be implied that all law breakers are demonic anyway. Being that the Creator has sanctioned the severity of their diabolical behavior, their problems are deserved. Such a viewpoint first ignores that a person's natural inclination is to bring forth a fundamental change in all of his or hers life. Secondly, the state has a lawful responsibility to offer adequate programming opportunities in areas of societal dysfunstioning, when its' citizens are rendered incapable, impoverished, incompetent, etc.. This responsibility exists despite where the origin of the dysfunction lies.

The mainstream society is evolving at a rate of great impetus. However, rehabilitation methods are still fixed in a position of stagnation, resulting in rates of recidivism skyrocketing while rates of successful re-entry plummet. This being the case, the future concerning recidivism and re-entry rates will be determined by whether the design of the criminal justice system's rehabilitation effort is revitalized and strengthened, or not.

Sincerely,
Maurice

While these classes had some really good points to them, they were also frustrating. I faced a lot of feelings of hopelessness when it came to our country wanting to reform the prison system. I mention President Obama here, and his decision to buy the Thomson Correctional Center in Illinois. Sure, there are studies going on about prison reform, and yes, there are programs like Inside-Out. But it still seems that when it comes down to it, our government likes to spend money putting people behind bars way more than on figuring out how to keep them outside those bars.

Co-author's note

The purchase of the Thomson Correctional facility is the perfect example of the long history of priority placed on the Prison Industrial Complex in this country. This purchase caused much controversy, but mostly because political leaders were concerned that it might house Guantanamo Bay prisoners – an idea that the administration had floated back in 2009. Once it was made clear that only U.S. prisoners would be destined for the jail cells, the sale was approved by Congress.[6]

The U.S. attorney general was appointed to oversee these classes. Part of the Justice Department's mission is supposedly to help previously incarcerated people after their release, so they sponsor a program dedicated to preventing recidivism. This class I was taking was a part of all that. Eric Holder was the attorney at the time. The model was a challenge, though, because there were so many people involved. We had the professor; then the unit manager – kind of like a case manager; there was executive staff; the warden; and then a federal official. Not to mention the university people who were running it. Every one of them had some say over the program. That's too many people with too many opinions, far as I can tell.

This letter is about me sharing some frustrations about the class, and even about the professor's approach sometimes. I mean, we students were asked to spill everything, tell the stories of our messed-up lives. Those were some rough tales. Then the professor just goes ahead and basically says at the end of all this something like: *You all have a chance to make things right now.*

So matter of fact, like we were just going to magically re-enter society and be greeted with open arms, good jobs, and no temptations from the people, the streets, and the situations that got us there in the first place. She knew better than that.

I was kind of asking in this letter: *What about the past generations?* What about all the stuff that caused our mess in the first place? We were casualties of a long history of societal war; it was about way more than one group of prisoners. But most of those people running the class wanted things to look good in the moment, without thinking about how their own responsibilities contributed to so many failures. I mean, they already knew all these things we were telling them; our stories were like sequels to past prisoner stories. The leaders had heard this stuff before, believe me, the poverty, drugs, and disease that made up so many of our lives. There was just no reality check going on and it got me mad. Just more of the same from prison staff, like, *Good luck out there.* Someone needed to face some truths. That's what my letter was about.

One more thing

November 15, 2013

Professor K,

Do you agree that the African-American who grows up in the bowels of those ghetto streets can be labeled as a modern day peasant? Can they be considered one of those who are part of today's version of American colonialism? For now, try to disregard any theory as to how this came to be. The fact is, those who live in a colonial condition will perfectly evolve within the boundaries set by a colonized mind set. Do you agree?

Are you aware that this mind set also establishes, in us, a colony which is fortified to protect the, "us" versus "them" philosophy, which exists in every aspect of our social relations?

Unfortunately, in the ghetto colony, we grow up engaging in a vicious cycle of hopelessness or mediocrity. On the surface, this may appear to define some of the anti-social behavior patterns, which can, at times, suggest an uncivilized culture. Obviously, being civil does exist, though it is in the perspective of the cycle. It, thereby, makes the harshness of our judgements irrational and lacking in intellectual insight.

I can relate as to why these theories (labeling, strain, disorganizational), are being tested by sociologists. But, at the conclusion of these findings, there isn't any more of a concentrated effort in bettering the conditions of their host.

Sincerely,
Maurice

This letter was just for my professor, it wasn't an assignment. She could be pretty raw sometimes; like I said, she had been incarcerated herself. One day in class, she started cussing at us. She said we were moving too slow, that people were holding out, feeling each other out too much. We were still in ice-breaker mode she said, and everything was taking too long to come out. After that we pulled out the guns, so to speak, and started shooting! You want to hear about what I think about colonialism? Well, okay then! We had some opinions and we just started sharing and speaking real talk after that.

I felt kind of bad for the college students who had signed up for this class sometimes. Maybe that's why we had been taking our time to come out with our stuff – we didn't want to scare them away. But then again, they signed up for it. We prisoners were at war and those students were going to have to toughen up if they wanted to be with us. They ended up loving the class, most of them. It was like they were thirsty for what happened in there. Nobody dropped out (I was a little surprised by that). Maybe we underestimated them. They came to trust us, and that's how they came to the understandings they did about what we had gone through, outside and inside of prison. They never heard stories like that before and it changed a lot of them. They started talking about wanting to be public defenders and everything.

The second part of this course was different, more like a think tank. The next level up. The college students were still participating, from campus this time. And it was our job to work with the prison administration to keep things going. We got them to agree to open Resource Centers in every unit – I ran the one in mine. These were like small libraries. People who were about to go home, for example, could do job searches on the computers there. I taught some classes at my center, like Critical Thinking, Writing, and African-American studies. The prison provided a curriculum, but I rarely followed it.

December 5, 2013

Professor,

Understanding the mechanism through which an imprisoned individual seeks escape through the use of narcotics and/or alcohol while he is behind prison walls is of paramount importance. Whether the behavior is caused by a pre-imprisoned mental disorder or is due to an acute addictive behavior of some sort, there are principals involved that are followed with certainty by the body of those that are confined.

In reference to myself, I can remember the informality that was ensured, on an autumn day, as I was sanctioned by the administration and sent to solitary confinement. It was there that one of my isolated neighbors and I spoke daily about how we could condition our minds to obtain a comfortable state while dwelling in the deepest section of the prison's inhumane design, The Hole. He replied; "sure, that's whats up, send your line over so that I can hook the literature up for you to review". When I pulled in the line, I retrieved the literature and was surprised to see the tiny, revised version of a King James Holy Bible. When I stated that I never thought that he was a Christian, he flatly responded with; "me neither". He requested that I go to Chapter 1, John, verses 36 thru 38. There I would find the details of his acquired belief system.

After finding the chapter that he directed me too and before I could utter a single word, I stared, muddled, for several minutes. The silence of my neighbor was considered a prisoner to prisoner encouragement. All would be well with what was laid in front of me. It was in this moment that l truly began to take a real look into the patterns of my mind and my behavior. There, the imbalances of my mental health had been completely exposed. As I sat there, watching the outfit* and substance, I strangely felt that I was having an epithany about what my father had said to me on the night of his death. "I'm tired Son". As my thoughts were correlating those words with my current situation, I began to feel the mental and spiritual exhaustion of my historical journey, present circumstance, and the toll all of it was having on me. The whole scene made sense. I rationalized that if I where to die here of an overdose it would yet, be considered, a win-win situation. I could exonerate myself from the charged offense of murder by the government and, perhaps, dwell in the comfort of the spiritual resting place of my father and grandmother.

I did follow the principles of those who are confined. After receiving a few brief directions from my neighbor, I became addicted to heroin for the next ten years of my imprisonment, though I never overdosed.

Thank you 'for your time, professor...

Sincerely,
Maurice

* Syringe

(Behind the scene)

It is no secret that mild torture and retaliation tactics are partakened within the walls of prisons. Prior to having major heart surgery I was forced to file an inmate grievance report against two medical transport officers for dishonestly and prematurely removing me from a scheduled catheter exam at a local hospital.

After being rescheduled and allowed to undergo the pro-cedure a week later, it was discovered that I had had (3) severely blocked arteries.

The letter to my professor gives another perspective on what I have written about before – my heroin addiction in prison. I felt

Figure 3. Certificate of Achievement upon completion of Inside Out Program

like sharing it with her, knowing she could relate. She had spent some time in that world, too. I never got responses back, by the way, because she was not allowed to correspond with us on a personal basis.

I put the "Behind the Scene" right after the letter because as soon as I graduated from that class was when my heart issues started coming on bad. I ended up in surgery and then took a long time to recover. So it took me a while to get back to running the Resource Center and all that kind of activity. There is more about this in the Epilogue, as well as what I referenced already in past letters. Let's just say that what I went through was medical torture, nothing less.

Co-author's note

Recently, *More Than Our Crimes* shared testimonies in their newsletter from prisoners inside Hazelton, where Maurice began receiving his subpar medical care for heart disease. As Pam Bailey, co-founder of the organization, writes: "Medical care — both lack of and poor quality — is the one of the most common topics of complaints that we hear from people confined in federal prison." One prisoner, named Damen, explained:

> Over the past 10 years, it's gotten bad. A specialist who came to the prison said I needed surgery on my neck and lower back and if I didn't get it I'd wake up one day paralyzed. He ordered an MRI and I was approved, but then I was denied because they didn't want to take me on the trip. To cover for it, one of the medical personnel tried to get me to sign a refusal form. I told him I would never do that...I need this MRI. I can't see a neurologist or get surgery without it.[7]

This is reminiscent of the experiences Maurice had at Hazelton. There's a helplessness that can descend upon an incarcerated patient, with so many roadblocks placed in their way. And filing complaints against prison protocol or staff can often be met with penalties ranging from denial of extracurricular activities to violence. This situation often turns into a vicious cycle resulting in desperation for the inmate.

In March 2023, *The Harvard Gazette* published an article on the present legal issues behind medical care in prisons. There is rising concern among scholars and reformists that the Supreme Court could strike down a previous ruling that established protections of the rights of prisoners in need of medical attention. Professor of Law, Crystal S. Yang, stated:

> The landmark Supreme Court case Estelle v. Gamble established that failure to provide adequate medical care to incarcerated people as a result of deliberate indifference to serious medical needs violates the Eighth Amendment's prohibition against cruel and unusual punishment. But…it is difficult for incarcerated individuals to bring lawsuits. Under the Prison Litigation Reform Act [PLRA], enacted in 1996, incarcerated individuals must meet certain requirements before they can file suit. For example, the PLRA requires incarcerated individuals to exhaust all administrative remedies by going through a correctional facility's internal grievance policies.[8]

Maurice, along with so many others, can testify to the ineffectiveness of "administrative remedies."

```
June 30, 2014

Professor K,

Greetings distinctive preceptress….

There are many accusations floating around
concerning the nature of prisoners. While
some are conveniently dressed in truth,
there are others that are stereo-typical and
misleading. Though these accusations range
from homosexuals and drug addicts to us
being simply plain ole evil-doers, none are
aimed at the center of placing imprisonment
in its proper perspective to repair its
```

over populated system, or extinguish its theoretical allegations. Although, one rather practical view is that, prison is nothing more than a sub-society, which depicts the same realities that are present within the mainstream society for which it has daily interaction.

As in the mainstream society, there are also very high rates of social diseases such as AIDS, hepatitis, and cancer, to stress induced issues such as obesity, which by its nature produces diseases like, hypertension, diabetes, or high cholesterol. But, there is one unprecedented ecliptic that proceeds in predominance all of these illnesses combined. I have never observed, visually or physically, the profoundly overlooked illnesses in the mental health variables.

There are a multitude of citizens being murdered, exploited, ostracized, miseducated, misdiagnosed, raped, and wrongfully judged for the inability to control their very own mind.

I have learned that the greatest harm which is being afforded to the well-being of us, the people of mental instability, is its mistreatment by our so-called mentally stable. Though it is their disregard for dissimilarity which perpetuates their lack in placing these illnesses of the people in a social proper prospective, I strongly consider that, we all suffer from a significant amount of mental instability. What do you feel about this particular analogy professor?

I cannot remember a period in my life where I was not incoherent to some degree or another. Added to the equation growing up in the disfunctions which accompany poverty, mental instability became the authority of the day.

I've had many forms of mental health issues throughout my lifetime, for which I also needed to apply several different methods to combat these authorities from taking full control of my psyche. I could honestly write that, it was because of this inability to detect what was truly wrong with me which led to so much of my turmoil in life.

For a long time it started out as basic depression, which activated many suicidal thoughts and actions (e.g., pilldropping, pistols in the mouth, etc.). But, that which caused me to become utterly concerned was when a mild version of schizaphrenia started to creep into my head. Images which I couldn't make out, loud voices yelling in my head when there was absolutely no one around, and paranoia of people's intentions toward myself. In the respective culture which I am from, there is a very thin distinction between suicide and homicide. They can be one and the same, or one can surely lead to the other.

Interpreting the labyrinths of the mind for some, can be a task which can produce grave results, especially as in my case where it had to be deciphered without the assistance of an administrator, or administered medication. This remoteness renders itself brutal onto an individual, whether imprisoned, or otherwise.

In light of a societal perspective, the significance of this lies in the fact that our minds are our greatest assets. Everything that is relevant to the evolutionary process in a society's stability we owe to the responsiveness of our mind's health.

I conclude with, if we do not invest all of our resources into the fitness of the mental health illnesses, life in these societies will continue to perpetuate injustices and grave intrusions to persist. Its continuity will wrongfully imply that, the mere law breaker is nothing more than an evil-doer.

And, our miseducated shall be isolated, and our misdiag-nosed are to be blamed.

Considering already that, our terminally ill are made to be the shallow spot in the balance of social spending, and shall be required to hold their end of the economy without any support, and our exploited spectrum should simply be the problem of the society.

Obviously, these injustices transfers themselves onto every aspect of our living, thereby my dear professor, I humbly plead that we let our societal covenant first be the honor of the health of the mind for all.

Sincerely,
Maurice

The biggest problem I had with this class, and most programs and people from prison, is there was not enough attention paid to mental health issues, as I write about in my essay at the end of this book. This class didn't address this enough; it wasn't a focus even though it should have been. Everything was about looking at the outward world, society, etc. But what we have inside of us, as I have written, makes us do a lot of what happens out there in that world.

This is the point in me writing this book – to push the subject of mental health to the center of the discussion about our prison system. Until we talk about this, all the rest of the stuff that people do is like Band-Aids on a wound. There will be no healing until this issue is as commonly discussed as the riots, food, and guards found inside. That is the prison reform I'm looking to hear about. Everything else will fall under that umbrella.

December 5, 2013

To Whom It May Concern,

I am writing this letter in recognition of Maurice W. Tyree achievements in completing the Inside-Out Prison Exchange Program that was held in the Fall of 2013 in the Hazelton United States Penitentiary. West Virginia University and USP Hazelton joined together to put forth another ground breaking program that will have lasting positive effects on all participants.

The Inside-Out Prison Exchange Program is a national program based in Philadelphia, Pennsylvania, at Temple University. The program was established in 1997 with the premise of bringing college students and incarcerated men and women together to explore and learn about issues of crime and justice from behind prison walls. The program was founded on the theory that incarcerated men and women and college students might mutually benefit from studying together as peers. To date, over 200 instructors have been certified to teach inside out from over 120 colleges and universities and also in other countries.

The men that participated in this program put forth an insurmountable degree of effort that separated them from all others. The Inside and Outside students were personally chosen by West Virginia University and Warden O'Brien. The Inside students were chosen due to their standing within the population as they were and are considered leaders. Maurice W. Tyree deserves to be personally recognized for not only the successful completion of this course but also his willingness to stand for the change this program represents.

The possibilities are endless with the participation of individuals that are willing to see a vision of positive change.

Thank you,

Jeri Kirby, M.A.
Inside-Out Facilitator
West Virginia University Faculty Instructor
Sociology and Anthropology

Figure 4. Confirmation Letter, Inside-Out Prison Education Program, West Virginia University

5
Letter of resignation

<u>Epilogue</u>

A LETTER OF RESIGNATION

To: My mind. My body.

My spirit. My Soul!

Beginning at this very moment, the junction contempted of the before and moored into the hereafter, I am drafting a letter unto myself. A 'letter of resignation' to my previous thoughts-to-actions and the invalid receptivity within my senses, to always behold a reminder of that which I could never result to become ever again.

I hereby submit this letter to and of, myself, in order to give notice of resignation to the output and intake to, blanket indictments of inferiority, self-hate, ingratitude, meaninglessness, and reasons thereof;

Surely, it is not my role to judge harshly nor inaccurately accuse myself. However, as once we had established a bond, in thought and behavior, I feel that it is only befitting to state the basis of my new aim as well.

I choose, by intent, to sever all remaining acts with you, for it was at the behest of decades of unconscious self-hatred, and childishness, in peculiar evironments, and pressures that have forced my acquiring of a new outlook and formal undertaking. We both should have known that to be a responsible person we should have thought more critical to hold others and ourselves to the standards required to solidify a self-loving and mature lifestyle.

By doing such, we uphold the unwavering legacy of our devoted ancestors, whom long standing bravery led them to a disciplined and communal way of life. It is within this line of acknowledgment that we show our gratitude to our existence, and honor their 500 plus years of racial tensions and revolutions.

This is not a scribe with self-condemnation thought, it is my written draft of, adolescence termination. Perhaps it saddens the souls of our ancestors, while staining their struggles with our defective values and vices. This places a blur upon their inspirited envisions.

This first, and most abhorrent among these vices is our daily denial of the existing fortunes that we've inherited through the unimaginable sacrifices, bloodshed, and deaths, such as, freedoms to exert our humanity (i.e. to speak, to look, to engage, to think, to read, to suggest, to be). They found and suffered appropriately in attempt to turn these envisions into an engrossed and manifested reality while we are an infallious enemy to our very own birthright.

Second, the private and public methods in which we commit blasphemy. Our thoughts, actions, and acculturations are culturally abnormal and less than dignified. It is by the inadequacy of these displays that generation after generation is being deprived and misled from their portion of that which is rightfully theirs, and ultimately an obstruction to their future investments. This is, ecological treason. And is greatly frowned upon in the policies of our ancestral creed. No matter how low we may decrease in social status, or what form our human diversity may take, our inherited oblige must remain intacted while prevailing over all else.

Thirdly, I lobby a charge against us of utter offense; it is the lack of, focus and personal investment. All the available resources and energy that's being invested into vice should be spent on the harmonization of our physical, mental, and spiritual liberation, to further our advances in becoming a solid man, and subsequently a competitive culture and people. To not see such waste or time as an act of suicide propels a charge accompanied by great consequences.

I conclude, there is not a man, not a woman who is not flawed in some way or another, and requires their fair share of adjustment. Nevertheless, ingratitude, vice, and/or self-hatred are things we can control. Knowing this is a lack of self-control which hinders our progress is why my departure is sound. We shall never deliberately forfeit that which protects us. Such intoxications must be overcome, and the obligation to policy, dictated upon us, long before our birth, must be re-established. If, only for the future's reference, we must be held accountable today for our offspring's survival tomorrow."

Farewell,

Maurice

A Black Oath: A Pledge of Allegiance for Black People by Dr. Frances Cress Welsing[1]

I Pledge Allegiance To My Own Black Self-Respect/
And To The Respect Of All Other Black/
(And Shades Of Black)/
People On Planet Earth,/
All Of Whom Are Victims Of The System Of Racism (White Supremacy)/
And I Pledge To Use All Of My Life Energy, Intelligence And Creativity,/
In All Areas Of People Activity,/
To Eliminate The Global System Of Racism (White Supremacy)/
On Planet Earth And To Replace It With Justice,/
So That There Can Be Peace,/
So Help Me God.

I copied this oath down and hung it on the wall in my cell. I don't know when I wrote it out exactly. It had to have been 'one of those days,' but I can't remember what happened on *that* day to have made me do this. Among all my papers I had – and there were a lot – I made sure this got saved. Even before all my legal documents. I laminated it so it couldn't be destroyed, which takes a lot to get something like that done in prison. You have to know somebody who knows somebody, like that.

I hung this on the wall of my cell, so I could look at it every day. It was there to keep me going, to save myself really. It was one of those "never forget" kind of things. The resignation letter I wrote

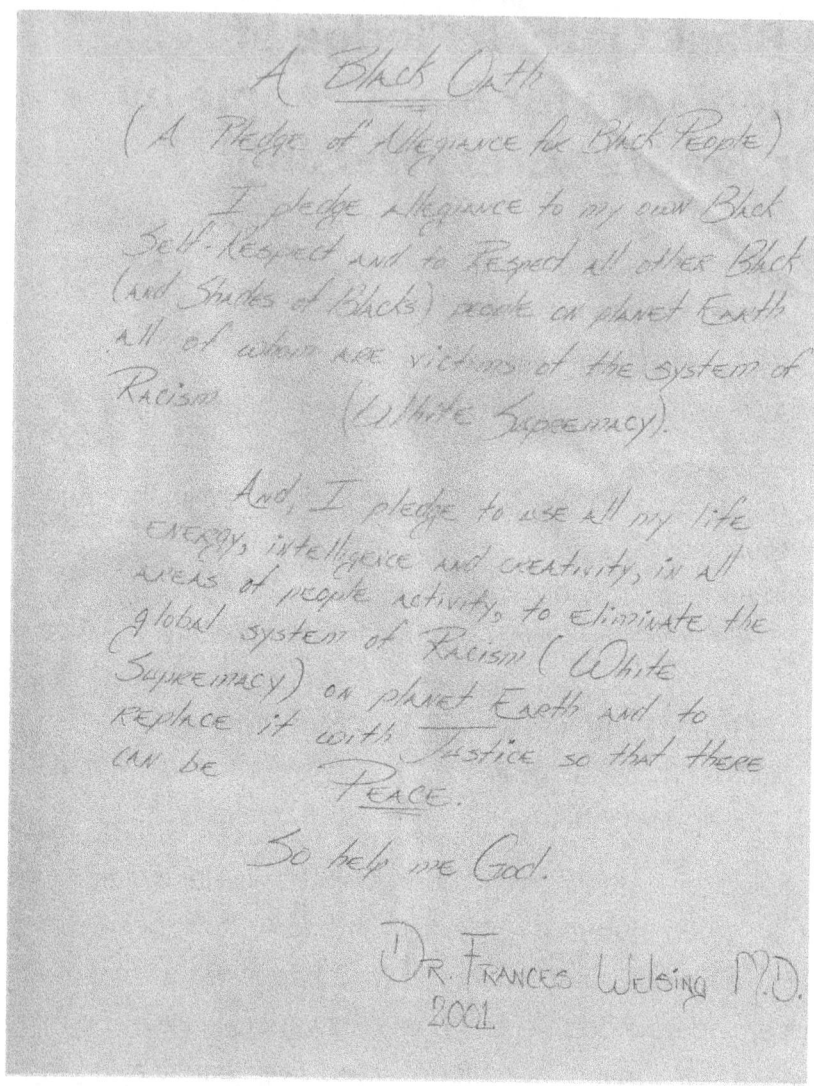

Figure 4. Author's handwritten "A Black Oath"

was in response to that oath. Dr. Cress Welsing's words had resonated with me and propelled me to write my own oath in the form of a letter. It was another step in my self-hatred discovery. That is what happens when you start reading the writings and hearing the stories of the people that come before you. You discover truths about yourself that you never knew existed. I had discovered that I hated myself, as well as other Blacks in general. I also discovered that there is a system in place outside of myself which birthed this degradation within me. It is kept well-nourished throughout society.

I had also read Dr. Welsing's *The Isis Papers* earlier on in my incarceration. She was a psychiatrist who formulated theories about humanity and went so far left, so independent, that numerous people in her field wouldn't accept her. This is the kind of book a lot of people weren't ready for, but I had already been looking into that field of study so I was more prepared. Your skin has to be tough to read things like what she wrote, they were controversial. Problem is, we get stuck on the little things other people say, so we don't have to look at the big picture, the actual issues.

Maybe some of the Dr.'s perspectives were a little excessive, but her point was there is some kind of racial wound in society that's not healing. And one of the reasons it won't heal is that – in my opinion – a lot of white people don't like Black people. And seeing as how white people are still in charge of pretty much everything, that's a problem. This is not an excuse. You can see in my letter that I don't make excuses. But it is an explanation. It is something that needs to be pointed out and looked at if we are trying to figure out how to fix things, like prisons. I'm not saying everything is about race inside, but it is about power – getting it and keeping it. And race is going to play a part in that dialectic no matter the situation.

Co-author's note

According to *Washington Post* reporter, Edward D. Sargent, Dr. Frances Cress Welsing "fits into that special mold of people who dare to study, research and come up with new conclusions about what reality really is." As Maurice expresses, one has to have a certain type of skin to be willing to face 'daring' conclusions. Welsing's most famous principle is the Cress Theory on Color Confrontation. As stated in her 1991 book, *The Isis (Yssis) papers: the keys to the colors:*

> The thrust towards superiority over peoples of color, the drive towards material accumulation, the drive towards a technological culture and the drive towards power are all cornerstones of the universal white supremacy culture, and they are viewed-in terms of the Color-Confrontation thesis -as responses to the core psychological sense of inadequacy. ... it is an inadequacy rooted in the inability to produce melanin. This genetic state is, in actuality, a variant of albinism.[2]

Welsing also argues that the fact that white people are in the minority contributes to a "numerical inadequacy" intrinsic to their being. In 1980 the journalist, Sargent, attended a conference where Welsing spoke about Black relationships. It quickly became about much more than that, Sargent writes. It was broadly about navigating a world dominated by whiteness, by racism:

> Racism obviously has spawned many of the societal problems -- including poor housing, poor education and unemployment -- which directly and indirectly result in much of the frustration among blacks, which

in turn drives black people to misplace their aggression and become destructive towards themselves and each other. Welsing wants to show black people that they need not blame themselves for being victims of a system and culture set up to perpetuate white supremacy.[3]

We can see in Maurice's writing the direct and indirect influences of Welsing's argument: Black people are tearing themselves down in a misguided attempt to destroy that which is holding them down. And, as he says in this letter, he won't judge himself "harshly nor inaccurately", but he's not making excuses either. Instead, he points to the systemic issues of our society that contribute so greatly to the dysfunction of its citizens and swears to himself that he will do everything in his power to no longer fall prey to them.

Those who see Welsing's thesis as important and groundbreaking argue that she is one of the first to look at the deviations of the white race, as opposed to focusing on the victimhood of the Black person. All of this, they claim, is with an eye towards treating the mental health of the African American – a focus sorely lacking in so much of the work being done. Maurice is not alone in feeling some connection with the psychiatrist's ideas. In 1990 the band, *Public Enemy*, sent out a pamphlet of Welsing's "Cress theory on color confrontation" as promotional material alongside their new album, *Fear of a Black Planet*. Their music has allusions to her work, they explained. They wanted people to understand where they were coming from, too.

My letter, like the oath, is directed to Black people, a Black person, me. I came to realize that I had not taken advantage of what the ancestors had made available for me. But you just don't know all that exists when you grow up a certain kind of way – it actually seems as if you inherited nothing. And this is the conflict, that lack of knowledge. So that's why I won't be too hard on myself.

What I learned after a while in prison, after a lot of reading and thinking, was that I can speak the way I want to because of the bloodshed of my forbearers. The martyrs. Like Dr. Martin Luther King, Jr. You grow up thinking these things are a given, but the fact is we should be grateful we can vote. Somebody laid that down for us, it wasn't something we earned on our own. I mean how could I go on disrespecting everything Dr. King did when I think of what I can do because of him and all the freedom fighters? It's like committing treason. I don't have to agree with him on everything, but I have to respect him for what he did for us.

Our ancestors are also the people close to us, like mothers and fathers. Not holding them in high esteem is disrespectful, too. That disrespect then brushes off onto the disrespector. It's a vicious cycle. Our parents, all of them, went through a lot. To disregard that and judge them for their actions, like there was no reason behind them, that's a bad habit to get into. I had a lot of bad habits at one time, and I needed to resign from them. I had been investing in individual activities, like crime, instead of working for our collective good. That had to stop. This letter was my suicide note because I was ready to kill that old me off.

I really recommend this letter-writing process, depending on where you're at. Truth is, most of us have things that need to die. I can't recall for sure, but it's more than likely that I shared this with other people in prison. As I mentioned, there was a lot of exchanging of writing there. And lots of commentary and feedback, too. All of it was therapy for me, like a diary. I started self-diagnosing after I realized nobody else was going to be checking in on the mental health of us prisoners. I prescribed to myself reading, writing, and talking about what I was thinking. But never did I think it would end up in a copyrighted book.

6
"Mental health's undocumented and oppressive continuum"

THE ACCUMULATION OF TRAUMA, UPON AN AFRICAN AMERICAN MALE, WITHIN THE FEDERAL BUREAU OF PRISONS

MENTAL HEALTH'S UNDOCUMENTED AND OPPRESSIVE CONINUUM

by

Maurice W. Tyree

<u>TABLE OF CONTENTS</u>

Introduction (Problem)   Pgs. 1-3

Forward I. (Declaration)   Pgs. 3-4

Section I. (Sexual Misconduct)   Pgs. 4-6

Forward II. (My Society's Forgiveness)   Pgs. 7-11

Section II. (Inadequate Medical Care)   Pgs. 12-15

Forward III. (Visitor)   Pgs. 16-18

Section III. (Visitation Regulations)   Pgs. 19-25

Conclusion (Solution)   Pgs. 26-30

Appendix

INTRODUCTION

What is trauma? The Webster's II, New Riverside University dictionary defined it as; **1.** An emotional shock that creates substantial and lasting damage to the psychological development of the individual, generally leading to neurosis. 2. Something that severely jars the mind or emotion.

What *is* bondage? Also, defined in Webster's as; 1. The condition of a *slave* or serf: Servitude; implies being owned *as* a possession or being treated as property. **2.** Subjection to power, force, or influence.

What I find most contextual and appropriate for this summation is the explanation of both ideologies given by, Dr. Joy A. Degruy, Ph.D in her book entitled "*Post* Traumatic Slave Syndrome: America's Legacy of Enduring Injury and Healing", which states;

"Trauma is an injury caused by an outside, usually violent, force, event or experience. We can experience *this* injury physically, emotionally, psychologically and/or spiritually. Trauma can upset *our* equilibrium and sense of well being. If a trauma is severe enough it can distort our attitudes and beliefs. Such distortions often result in dysfunctional behaviors, which can in turn, produce unwanted consequences. If one traumatic experience can result in distorted pattern is magnified exponentially when a person repeatedly experiences severe trauma, and it is much worse when the traumas are caused by human beings."

She goes on to simplify bondage by stating;

"Bondage is antithetical to humanity. Therefore, bondage in any form is abusive. When we discuss living in bondage, we are discussing only degrees of abuse."

I firmly observe and experience a concerted effort of a prison bureaucracy who's singular mission is to promote a coercive system and systematically corrosive environment where the individual is marginalized, while at the same time dehumanized, to such an extent, that all sense of self worth and hope is obliterated.

It is my intention, that the proceeding text, as well as, the enclosed documents will present a comprehensive and unquestionable litany of evidence, that the United States, Bureau of Prisons' continually campaigns to eradicate any form of legitimate protestation or challenge, by inmates seeking redress and remedy for concerns and grievances. I will endeavor to cast a spotlight upon a system which is dismally failing, and is viewed by many progressive penologists, as an entity, who continuously, and with purpose of conscious denies quality medical care, inhabitable and productive work environments, and promotion of strong family and friend ties. Thereby leaving the incarcerated little to no opportunity for rehabilitation, thus 5ignificantly reducing successful reintegration back into society. The direct result, "The Industrial Prison Revolving Door Dilemma."

What is to follow is a chronological account of questionable steps taken by the Bureau of Prisons to ensure the individual is placed in a position where they find themselves denied mandated services, abandoned without the expectation of resolution, while contradicting, and at times ignoring it's own established policies.

FORWARD I. (DECLARATION)

It is, quite certain, that I have played a destructive role, in the suffering of my community, on account of the suffering of my society. I have, in an innate manner, expressed atonement with the creator, my family, the highest governing office in the land, The White House, and myself. Therefore, in a much progressive light, I must filter the suffering of my society to aid in it's healing, even in the expenditure of my mind. I accept, and will endure my tribulations to replenish the characteristics of my community.

As a social peer, a black male in that peerage, and human being, I want (to obtain) the meaning of the things that have shape my condition, which presently drives my thoughts, both good and bad. I want (to redeem), if you will, the garbage of my existence, to allow the course which will strengthen it's quality. A maximum redemption of something lost, that will place meaning back where there is no deadness. Not merely to reproduce a dramatization to an experience, but to put something additional, which was ·overlooked in an experience. Perhaps more context, or more gravity in the particulars.

Or messages that reflect things already known and written about repetitiously to the general public, and, the individual soul.

Maurice Tyree

SECTION I.

<u>115.11 Zero tolerance of sexual abuse and sexual harassment</u>; An agency shall have a written policy mandating zero tolerance toward all forms of sexual abuse and sexual harassment, and outlining the agency's approach to preventing, detecting, and responding to such conduct. Victims of sexually abusive behavior and sexual harassment should receive, timely and effective <u>responses</u> <u>to</u> <u>their</u> <u>physical, psychological,</u> and <u>security</u> <u>needs</u>;

In April of 2015, I was transferred from Hazelton's United States Penitentiary (U.S.P) to Butner's Federal Correctional Institution 2 (F.C.I 2).

Shortly after my transfer I was given a position in Unicor, the institution's clothing manufacturing plant. By August of 2015, due to a working environment, which had become increasingly untenable, as well as emotionally uncomfortable, I was compelled to resign my position as a Quality Assurance Inspector, within Unicor.

The reason behind my self termination was due to a specific staff member, who created an atmosphere which was rife with lewd and suggestive sexual gestures, and sexually explicit language.

Before leaving Unicor, I attempted on several occasions to bring my concerns to a number of staff members, which included, Ms. Mutchec (Unicor Factory Manager), Mr. J. Baskerville (Unit Counselor), Ms. T. Ralfelt (Unit Case Mahager), and D. Muhammed (institution's chaplain). Only to find my concerns dismissed, and failed to be reported to the institution's appropriate department, or the Bureau of Prisons' agency or agencies set in place for such matters. (see attached documents)

Feeling much like a victim of uncontrollable circumstances, I then realized that I was left with no other option but to leave my job. It was shortly after this decision that I began to reflect upon the circumstances, and I came to the conclusion, that I was not going to let the actions of others determine my faith. I therefore decided to petition the administration of Unicor to be reinstated to my former position. I was immediately informed that I would be placed on a waiting list, which could take up to a year for my return.

Almost a year later from the date I had resigned, and to my surprise, I received payment for hours worked in Unicor. Needless to say, I was somewhat perplexed, for I had of that date not been rehired, nor was this back pay. Upon further investigation, I learned that it was an oversight by the Unicor payroll department. It seemed the payroll department was under the idea that I was already working again in the Quality Assurance Department, then subsequently terminated, something that only staff are aware of, but failed to inform me of (see attached documents). This left me with the impression that once again Unicor was attempting to sabotage my livelihood, while decreasing my opportunities at gainful employment.

Unicor finally rehired me on 9/1/16. When I resumed working, I was informed that I would no longer be working in the Quality Assurance Department, but placed in the production department. Since my return to Unicor, there have been several interactions where staff have in no uncertain terms reminded me of my place and that of my former accusations.

I have not been reinstated within Unicor for ten months. During that time I have not had an incident or disciplinary report written. I further believe that I have deported myself in a respectful and professional manner. Therefore, I find it a sad commentary that an individual, who has limited resources and who's only desire is to be self supported and without conflict, has found in the past unwarranted obstacles and outrageous behavior by those officious individuals who laid their authority over those without the means of redress.

In conclusion, I have enclosed documentation which will add substance to my contention pertaining to this most unfortunate situation. I anticipate that you, like me, will find that this particular incident is an example of prison bureaucracy that has become a rudderless vessel, which is sinking due to it's own cumbersome weight of rhetorical hypocrisy and contradictions.

From: *Post Traumatic Slave Syndrome: America's Legacy of Enduring Injury and Healing*, by Joy DeGruy Leary:

> Trauma is an injury caused by an outside, usually violent, force, event or experience. We can experience this injury physically, emotionally, psychologically, and/or spiritually.

> Traumas can upset our equilibrium and sense of well-being. If a trauma is severe enough it can distort our attitudes and beliefs. Such distortions often result in dysfunctional behaviors, which can in turn produce unwanted consequences. If one traumatic experience can result in distorted attitudes, dysfunctional behaviors and unwanted consequences, this pattern is magnified exponentially when a person repeatedly experiences severe trauma, and it is much worse when the traumas are caused by human beings.[1]

I start this essay, which I wrote in 2017, defining some words I think are important for the discussion. There is *trauma* and there is *bondage*. In my case, and the case of so many other Black Americans, the two words are connected. What I want to provide here is testimony to the brokenness of the prison system. I want people to see the pattern of constant abuse that is nonstop in every department, and straight up the ladder.

The essay is a collection of pieces I wrote separately. Altogether it illustrates a system of exploitation. One day, in prison, I realized I had been documenting everything, and suddenly it all fell into place, into themes. That's when I envisioned this essay.

Co-author's note:

Maurice references a "Revolving Door Dilemma," in the essay. This is a phrase often used in discourse around the penal system. It is in fact, a theoretical framework in the analysis of recidivism. And, in the United States, we rank extremely high in recidivism rates. According to a recent study in the *Harvard Political Review*, "Within three years of their release, two out of three former prisoners are rearrested and more than 50% are incarcerated again."[2]

I'm starting in Section I with Part 115 of the *Prison Rape Elimination Act National Standards*. I looked it up on the Federal Bureau of Prisons web page. Here I'm telling the story of the sexual harassment I underwent while at my job in Butner. It was something I really didn't think to report at first. The work that it would have taken to go through all the channels of prison paperwork just seemed too much for me. But I was seeing a psychologist at the time, and she encouraged me to report the abuse. She was what they call a 'mandated reporter,' so she was going to have to report what I said if I didn't, but she wanted to give me the chance to do it myself. So many prison staff just brush stuff like this under the rug; it's usually more trouble than they think it's worth to follow up on prisoner complaints. But this doctor wasn't going to hide those reports I provided, she was actually going to submit them. What I am saying is she was a good person, doing her job, and I don't want it overlooked that there are good people who work for the Bureau of Prisons.

This reminds me of a nurse I once had in solitary confinement – another one of the good people. Miss Bradshaw was her name. I met her when I was in the SHU (Special Housing Unit). I was suffering from a hyperthyroid issue while I was in there, so they sent me a nurse. There are certain security issues in the hole – you can't just pop a cell open and walk on in. But Miss Bradshaw didn't care. In fact, a lot of times she didn't even bring the handcuffs. See, I was supposed to be getting some kind of protein drink, like Ensure, to make me strong enough to handle the medications I was getting for my medical issue. My body needed to bulk up some in order to handle the strong medication. I was pretty thin by that time. Well, because of budget cuts they told me that I wasn't going to get any. But Miss Bradshaw brought those drinks to me. She would smuggle them into my cell, in her uniform, pulling the cans out from all sorts of places – pockets, her bra. She actually cared, she saw me as a person. That stood out to me.

FORWARD II

"Give me your tired, your poor, your huddled masses yearning to breathe free, the wretched refuge of your teeming shore. Send these, the homeless, tempest tossed to me, I lift my lamp beside the golden door."

Dear Mr. and Mrs. Obama,

As always, I ask that the Universal Creator favor you and your administration and all that you hold dear and desire to accomplish in matters of prosperity.

It is with vested difficulty that I offer, to the both of you a brief letter on behalf of the African- American class that live in areas of America's inner cities popularly known as the ghettos. I write to you as a member of this group, which also includes my endeared family and friends who have also grown up and lived in this milieu of the Black poor.

First, however, I must submit an apology, publicly given, that demonstrates my great concern for how the framework of American society has been negatively impacted by the uncivil social relations that have existed for the past several decades or so. Specifically, I apologize for the role played by generations of my peers and fellow class members in creating that negative result.

Some of our past Black leaders and ancestors have suffered the ultimate sacrifice as a result of their support of our culture and causes. While I think they would wisely understand the reasons behind some of our questionable actions, I also believe that they would express shameful disappointment in the methods used.

I do not believe there has been an intentional attempt to disregard the progress of our society as much as there has been a lack of acknowledgment of it. Such progress has been repeatedly masked by the attention paid to crime, slothfulness, and other deviances that society, in general, has labeled us with. The evident fascination with such depictions have further obscured our progress, both as a people and as a culture. It is to the extent that members from our social class have committed, supported, and perpetuated these negative attributes that I offer an apology. Their actions have only reinforced a historical creed that can be said to have affected our peoples' spirit and has also resulted in the social rejection of our class. We have been ostracized and marginalized and this reality has almost become hereditary in nature as current generations are stigmatized with the same pariah social standing that has afflicted prior generations. This state of affairs is in direct contradiction to the intent and meaning behind the aphorism depicted on the Statue of Liberty.

Even after acknowledging the role our people have played in the creation of the current scenario, it is also true that our participation does not come close to completely explaining the current state of affairs. Other forces and segments of society have arguably contributed as much, if not more, to our plight. As a result they bear a corresponding amount of responsibility.

Your Honorable Governors, we are the infirm offspring that have been shaped by the impeachable sins of our birthplace's forefathers and by our own genealogical origins that have been influenced, as they were, by slavery and dehumanization. One result of the degradation we have suffered is that our culture, and the personality of our people, have been trivialized. Given society's infatuation with the perceived shortcomings of our existence, ie; broken families, disease and illness, mass incarceration, and high rates of unemployment, it is hard to grasp and reconcile the views that you, as leaders of American society, expound. The notions that the attainment of prosperity and the ideology, found in the United States constitution, that promises color blindness are fluttered before us as real when, in fact, they have been rendered unattainable by the very reality of our existence. To most of us these notions are but fragments of a daydream.

History teaches us that those who are included and made part of their society, through personal investment, will be better motivated to help sustain their society's well being and act, more concertedly and consciously, to defend and adhere to it's norms, values, and principles as opposed to rejecting them altogether. There is also a theory that is similar, but different, which suggests that no structure, social or otherwise, is ever whole when one of its' parts is omitted. The elevation of the whole will, inevitably be threatened by the decline of any of its' parts. Such a viewpoint would advocate that all citizens must be incorporated into society for that society to advance to its' fullest, or those excluded will be motivated and tend to work toward its' decline. It should come as no surprise then that the people of our class, for whom I am a matured model, have been effectively disenfranchised and excluded relative to participating in and receiving the benefits associated with full incorporation into American society.

I quote here, in part, from the Reverend Dr. Martin Luther King Jr.'s historic "I HAVE a Dream" speech, where, in front of 200,000 civil rights marchers, gathered at the steps of the Lincoln Memorial in Washington, D.C., he said on August 28, 1963; "negroes live on a lonely island of poverty in the midst of a vast ocean of material prosperity. 100 years later, the negro still is languished in the corner of American society, and finds himself in exile in his own land… When the architects of our Republic wrote the magnificent words of the constitution and Declaration of Independence, they were signing a promissory note to whichever Americans were to fall heir. This note was a promise that all men, yes, Black men as well as White men, would be guaranteed the unalienable right of life, liberty, and the pursuit of happiness".

These statements, by our beloved spiritual civil rights leader, are consistent with the present day conditions that reveal a truth that words simply cannot possible begin to explain.

Now, why do I see and express things in a certain light and have, instinctively felt a need to inform the highest office of our Country of its insight?

Yet again, it was stated better by our civil rights movement leader who addressed non-violent protests by demonstrators and Freedom Riders at Brown Chapel in Selma, Alabama on March 8, 1965: "deep down in our non-violent creed is the conviction…. that there are some things that are so dear, some things so precious, some things that are so eternally true that they are worth dying for, and if a man happens to be 36 years old, as I happen to be, and some great truth happens to stand before the door of his life, some great opportunity to stand up for that which is right, and he is afraid that his home will be bombed, or he will lose his job, or he will get shot, or beat down by state troopers, if he goes on to live until he is 80 years old, he is just as dead at 36, as he would be at 80. And, the sensation of breathing life is merely the belated announcement of an earlier death of the spirit….he died! A man dies when he refuses to stand up for that which he feels is right. A man dies when he refuses to stand up for justice. A man dies when he refuses to take a stand for that which is truth."

Mr. and Mrs. Obama, on behalf of my class and myself, I pose a question of great concern; what can be deployed to aid in the erection of a people whose heredity leads them to devalue their society?

I humbly conclude that, regardless of my classes' observations, our lives and freedoms do matter. They matter, not only for the cause of our human rights, but also for the empowerment of its' future generations' social health which, by its' nature, will determine the good health of the United States of America and ensure the fierce competitiveness that is warranted to maintain our country's standing on the world stage.

I humbly appreciate your time knowing that it is precious. For your consideration concerning my letter, I thank you in kindness.

Sincerely,
Maurice W. Tyree
August 18, 2015 FCI Butner 2, NC

I felt ignited, seeing a Black family in the White House. So many Black people were. And all that thinking I had been doing in prison, it needed to be shared with someone in power, someone who might understand a little something about what we were all going through. The election had sparked my interest – a lot of us followed the campaign. As soon as they won – and I do see it as the whole family being voted in – I made a vow to write the President. I also decided I would write every President after that, but I never did.

It was no bigger deal to write to the President than to anyone else from prison. I just put the letter in the regular mail with regular stamps. Of course, the officers have to read it first. I remember the one on duty who read this letter, Miss Smith. I saw a look on her face the next morning that said something like, *what in the hell are you even doing?* But they have to mail it. It's a federal offense to tamper with U.S. Mail, even when that mail comes from prisoners.

The apology part here is hard for some people to understand. Most of my brothers in prison didn't understand. They felt that

Obama should have known the problems we faced, that so much of our lives were never in our own hands – so why apologize for that? But what I say is there's still a need for accountability. So, I am apologizing in this letter for how we in the ghetto have responded to the circumstances we've been given. I mean I'm really apologizing to America through the office of the President. Remember, this letter was written before all these progressive narratives started coming out around the Black community; before the increased inner-city activism; before much attention was being paid to improve the lives of kids who grow up in violence. I knew what needed to happen, and you could say I was on it before a lot of other people were. There's got to be reform *and* there's got to be accountability – if things are really going to change.

Like I explained before, in prison we shared stuff with each other: personal letters, scholarly writings, things like that. And we are the most hostile critics of each other's work you're going to find. If you get a pass from a brother, then you know you pretty much made it, you said something important or meaningful. I didn't get a lot of passes on this letter. Besides the apology, they also couldn't understand why I didn't ask the President for anything – long as I was writing him anyway. A pardon or something. But I just wanted to talk, to rap with the President, Black man to Black man – tell him what was happening, in *my* language. That's what all my letters were, conversations I wanted to have that I couldn't have face to face. I was sequestered from people in all sorts of ways, hungry for discourse. Just like with all the other people I wrote, I was telling the Obamas: *Don't forget about me.* I was reminding people that just because they couldn't see me, didn't mean I wasn't there – and I wasn't thinking some big thoughts either.

When I said in this letter that some of our past Black leaders have suffered because of their support for the community, I am definitely talking about "Black on Black" crime. I know that's not popular to say. But what else are you going to call it when Black people cause violence against other Black people? I mean should it have another name? I know because the dominant society is white people, they see our crimes as different than theirs. So there's no one calling anything "white on white crime." But we all have the same issues, even if we don't see them the same way or call them the same thing. Race was created to separate. That's our history. So yes, I am saying it's sometimes risky to go into our community as one of us and try to help. That's just real life.

Don't misunderstand about the apology here, by the way. The issues that people like me face from the minute we're born *are* systemic. What I'm saying is that we don't have to agree to that system. That's what I'm apologizing for, not doing what I needed to do back then – the things I'm finally doing now. The letter is a threat in one kind of way. I'm apologizing to the world that I didn't have my head on straight then, and then telling them I do now. I am unbending my mind, and there's going to be a lot that comes from that, from me, because of that process. Not violence either. The opposite of violence: thought and action. That's the threat – watch out for me because I'm coming through with a new mind!

This makes me think of my experience with the Inside Out program again. Talking to the reps for the attorney general at that time, I tried to explain to them that taking that course – and doing all the other things I had to do just to get to participate – were all a means of teaching myself and my people how to eradicate the people running the operation in the first place. We have to eradicate the system, and they are participants in the system. If we as a people stopped joining in on the behavior that brings us so much trouble, then the system would be no more.

And all those people would be out of a job. So, in a way, *we* are the glue that keeps this destructive system together – even though it looks like it's all those officers, guards, cops and politicians who keep the wheels moving.

The Declaration of Independence says: "We hold these truths to be self-evident, that all men are created equal…" And the Constitution says: "All persons are equal before the law…" For some people, seeing a Black President in the White House was proof that this country stands by those claims. But most of us know that those are just words used to make it out to be *our* fault when we can't rise up by pulling on our bootstraps.

When I wrote that "No structure… is ever whole when one of its parts is omitted", it was something from the literature of the Inside Out program, out of Temple University. A body is still a body if it's missing a part, but it's an ailing body. That's how they explain the need for a healthy society. All parts of a body have to be functioning to be healthy. It's a concept that I write about a lot in my letters: the individual versus society. We live in an individualistic world instead of a humanistic one. People who look like me, who maybe have made mistakes (like I have), have struggled through rough times… they get put away – literally. And then, if we ever get let out, we are still put away in a sense, never embraced by the bigger society even though, supposedly, we have 'done our time'. How does that help humanity's progress?

Dr. Martin Luther King, Jr. spoke about Black disenfranchisement all the time. But we don't get taught those words of his as much as other ones. I quote his "I Have a Dream" speech in this letter, but it is a part a lot of us don't get taught. He started off by saying:

> But 100 years later, the Negro still is not free. One hundred years later, the life of the Negro is still sadly crippled by the manacles of segregation and the chains of discrimination. One hundred years later, the Negro lives on a lonely island of poverty in the midst of a vast ocean of material prosperity. One hundred years later, the Negro is still languished in the corners of American society and finds himself an exile in his own land. And so we've come here today to dramatize a shameful condition.[3]

We don't hear this part of the speech quoted a lot because it doesn't go with the story that says the Constitution and Declaration of Independence claim we're all equal, so we must be. No, Dr. King called out his country, but his words get hidden in his "dream". A dream is something unreal, something you might be wishing for. He's saying: *I have a dream that Black people will get equal treatment – because that's not what's happening right now*. It's still a dream, far as I can see.

I wrote this letter because I wanted to let the Obamas know that some of us "get it". The troubles are real for us, the system is against us, *and* we have to advance ourselves, too. But here's the problem: too many people are advancing from our misery, getting something off the backs of our disenfranchisement. That's the system, and I wanted him to know just what it looks like. If he is for real, I was thinking, then he would be able to address the situation. I mean he knows what it's like to get degraded right through the bloodline.

Of course, I would have loved to know what the Obamas thought about my words. But I also just liked the idea of them thinking about the questions. That was satisfying enough for me. I was motivated by spirit – it wasn't some kind of exchange thing. I really just wanted to say: *You were voted in as our first Black President. Everyone is vying for your Black perspective. But what about us, those people who won't be President, the ones that come from what people call 'the gutter'? Us folks who didn't even have the right to vote you into office? We're suffering here. What about **us** Black people and **our** perspective?*

I didn't need a response. Asking the questions I had been asking meant I was already making progress on my own, winding my way through the stupid stuff, knowing there was wisdom down the road. So, in the end, whether the president wrote me back or not isn't really the point. Like many of my letters, the point was about expressing myself in order to process and grow – to ultimately carry myself out of the depths I started in.

Co-author's note

On July 14, 2015, President Obama addressed the NAACP's 106th national convention in Philadelphia. The crux of his speech was prison reform. This was one month before Maurice wrote his letter to the Obamas.

In his speech, the president acknowledged as pertinent both personal accountability and the extant circumstances ripe for creating lives that end up committing crimes – the two points Maurice references in his letter. Addressing the inequity involved in living in America as a Black or brown person, President Obama said:

> By just about every measure, the life chances for black and Hispanic youth still lag far behind those of their white peers. Our kids, America's children, so often are isolated, without hope, less likely to graduate from high school, less likely to earn a college degree, less likely to be employed, less likely to have health insurance, less likely to own a home. Part of this is a legacy of hundreds of years of slavery and segregation, and structural inequalities that compounded over generations. It did not happen by accident. Partly it's a result of continuing, if sometimes more subtle, bigotry -- whether in who gets called back for a job interview, or who gets suspended from school, or what neighborhood you are able to rent an apartment in…

He also goes on to say: "There are a lot of folks who belong in prison… They may have had terrible things happen to them in their lives. We hold out the hope for redemption, but they've done some bad things…" As the lives of Maurice and so many others illustrate, it is crucial to hold out hope for those who have done "bad things".

From acknowledging the historical foundations of racism and bigotry, to asserting that some people do belong in prison – at least for the time being – the president finally calls out the fact that so many prisons are simply unfit for any human being, no matter their wrongdoing:

> …we want to be in a position in which if somebody in the midst of imprisonment recognizes the error of their ways, is in the process of reflecting about where they've been and where they should be going, we've got to make sure that they're in a position to make the turn. And that's why we should not tolerate conditions in prison that have no place in any civilized country. We should not be tolerating overcrowding in prison. We should not be tolerating gang activity in prison. We should not be tolerating rape in prison. And we shouldn't be making jokes about it in our popular culture. That's no joke. These things are unacceptable.[4]

Maurice, among so many others who are and have been incarcerated, has recognized the "errors of his ways", while at the same time recognizing just how broken the American prison system is. Both can be true.

The president announced to the NAACP crowd that he planned to visit a prison – the first sitting president ever to do so. Two days later he toured the El Reno prison, outside Oklahoma City. Meeting with several inmates, he told them it could just as easily have been him in there, were it not for the support he received from family and community.

During his time in office, President Obama made strides in prison reform, more than any other president in modern history – although the bar is certainly low on that. And it is evident that Obama was one of the few presidents actually interested in addressing this issue in any meaningful or sustained manner.

Perhaps his own identity as a Black man indeed fueled his interest in this institution that has historically flourished by punishing Black and brown men above all other Americans.

So why is it taking so long for leaders in the United States to seriously address prison reform, even as the movement writ large has been in motion since the early 1800s?

Undeniably, reforms have occurred but there is a difference between the enactment of policies and the consistent implementation of said policies. We know from the personal testimonies of so many incarcerated people that, among other issues, mental health care is sorely lacking in these places; that physical violence remains a constant part of life inside; and that the 'them-versus-us' paradigm is baked into the bureaucratic framework. We also know that for our political leaders, addressing this issue can be anathema to a political career – depending upon whose votes one is courting.

What does that look like in our contemporary leaders? In March 2023, President Biden signed a Republican-sponsored resolution blocking new Washington D.C. laws intended to overhaul the process of prosecuting and punishing crime. This was a bill that prison reformists were championing.

And then, of course, there's the notorious 1994 crime law (The Violent Crime Control and Law Enforcement Act) sponsored by then-Senator Biden and signed into law by President Bill Clinton. This was part of the continuing tough-on-crime stance, one shown to be a major factor in the grand rise of mass incarceration in this country – especially of Black and brown people. (To note, there are those who argue that the spike in incarceration did not directly correlate to this law – and that there were true reforms attached to it, such as the Violence Against Women Act). In his 1994 speech on the floor of the Senate, Biden said:

> Just like when I first got into politics...[I] ran on a law and order platform... Every time Richard Nixon, when he was running in 1972, would say "law and order," the Democratic match or response was law and order with *justice*, whatever that meant. And I would say, ``Lock the SOB's up.'...Because guess what? What has every major crime bill that has gotten this far been? A Democratic crime bill. A Democratic President wants 100,000 cops. A Democratic President wants to build 125,000 new prison cells. That is the secret."[5]

The secret being that both major political parties tend to capture more votes with hard-on-crime platforms than reformist approaches.

While President Biden has claimed a changed mind since the 1990s when it comes to crime and punishment, his decades-long involvement in locking up more people (not fewer), reflects our country's commitment to keeping criminals out of sight – and mind.

In a 1996 speech by Hilary Clinton, the then-First Lady, she uttered the infamous term, 'superpredator'. In championing her husband's signing of the 1994 crime bill, she said:

> Just as in a previous generation we had an organized effort against the mob. We need to take these people on. They are often connected to big drug cartels, they are not just gangs of kids anymore. They are often the

kinds of kids that are called superpredators — no conscience, no empathy. We can talk about why they ended up that way, but first, we have to bring them to heel.[6]

While there continues to be an argument as to whether Clinton was referencing African Americans specifically, what is clear is that she believed – at least at that time – that there were some people for whom there was no hope, no *correction* possible. They just did not have the same human characteristics that most of us do, thus it was rational to sentence them to a life of isolation that often included forced servitude, to heel at the feet of justice. We have been rationalizing this idea for centuries; old habits die hard.

In a 1998 *New Yorker* article, Toni Morrison called Bill Clinton the "first Black president." She described him as a "single-parent household, born poor, working-class, saxophone playing, McDonald's-and-junk-food-loving boy from Arkansas." One can take that as one chooses, but his popularity with African Americans got him into office – and kept him there for two terms. But calling him a friend to Black Americans might be misguided. Mass incarceration continued to increase for the next fourteen years after that 1994 bill was signed.

Clinton's willingness to carry the 'tough on crime' torch passed down to him by Presidents Reagan and Bush directly affected those he owed his campaign victories to.

The prison system has enjoyed strong support from American presidents since its inception in 1851. And no matter what some may no longer say out loud, that support is hardly waning. Whether it's President Herbert Hoover establishing the Bureau of Prisons (BOP) in 1930 or Richard Nixon establishing the 1971 zero-tolerance policy for drug-related crimes, our country continues to actively throw money and resources towards its prison system. And while prison reformists like Maurice abound, they often do not have the visibility and financial backing of those who would like to see the prison industrial complex continue to thrive. So, yes, individual accountability matters. But the system must be tamed, because all the self-reflection in the world on the part of those in crisis won't stop the voracious monster of a penal system that continues its feeding frenzy on this country's vulnerable citizens.

Section II: 2014 Hazelton, 2015 Butner

SECTION II

5310.17 <u>Elements of an adequate mental health care system</u>;

The Eighth Amendment requires that prison officials provide a system of ready access to adequate mental health care. First, there must be a systematic program for <u>screening</u> and <u>evaluating inmates</u> in order to identify those who require mental health treatment. Second, <u>treatment</u> <u>must</u> <u>entail</u> <u>more</u> <u>than</u> <u>segregation</u> <u>and</u> <u>close</u> <u>supervision</u> of the inmate patients. Third, treatment requires that the participation of trained mental health professionals, <u>who</u> <u>must</u> <u>be</u> <u>employed,</u> <u>in</u> <u>sufficient</u> <u>numbers</u> <u>to</u> <u>identify</u> <u>and</u> <u>treat</u> <u>in</u> <u>an</u> <u>individual</u> <u>manner</u> those treatable inmates suffering from serious mental disorders. Fourth, <u>accurate,</u> <u>complete,</u> <u>and confidential</u> <u>records</u> <u>of</u> <u>the</u> <u>mental</u> <u>health</u> <u>treatment</u> <u>process</u> <u>must</u> <u>be</u> <u>maintained.</u> Fifth, prescription and administration of behavior-altering medications in dangerous amounts, by dangerous methods, or without appropriate supervision and periodic evaluation, is an unacceptable method of treatment. Sixth, a basic program for the identification, treatment and supervision of inmates with suicidal tendencies is a necessary component <u>of</u> <u>any</u> <u>mental</u> <u>health</u> <u>treatment</u> <u>program.</u>

In 2014, during my 13th year in prison, I underwent triple bypass open heart surgery while incarcerated at Hazelton's United States Penitentiary (U.S.P.). After the surgery and the customary recovery period at the hospital, I was transferred back to the penitentiary and placed in the suicide watch section within the prison. During this time of extraordinary isolation, I was visited by several staff members of Hazelton's psychology department (Dr. Flanner and Dr. Ivory), who proceeded to inform me that my placement within the suicide watch area was due to overcrowding in the Special Housing Unit (S.H.U.), and not because of any complications from surgery or unresolved mental issues which might need resolving before my return to general population. I was to discover later that my placement in the suicide watch section, regardless of the S.H.U.'s overflow issue, was in direct conflict with stated policies, set forth by the Bureau of Prisons (B.O.P.), concerning guidelines pertaining to who may not be placed in said isolation. The only conclusion I could draw from this incident was that the Bureau of Prisons had violated it's own policy, and that the psychology department was complicit in this violation.

By 2015, a number of traumatic events had taken place that seemed to impede my recovery from coronary surgery. My sister passed away due from complications of AIDS. My grandmother, the kind and gentle soul who raised me, also passed on to her reward. My mother, who struggled with addiction for decades was diagnosed with HIV. Added to all this was the recurring years of attempting to reconcile the issues surrounding my father's violent heroin overdosing death.

All of these events created an atmosphere of overwhelming sadness and despair. I now found myself in a dilemma. I could slowly implode emotionally, or I could reach out and ask for help. Due to the feeling of being overwhelmed and under insurmountable stress, I decided to request an interview with the psychology department at Butner FCI 2.

In October 2015, I was granted an interview with Dr. Halbsgut, the attending psychologist. I entered into the session with a feeling of anticipation and elation, that finally, I was going to receive professional care and counsel for all of my concerns and woes. I was anticipating that the doctor would pose\appropriate analytical questions to determine what a proper therapeutic regimen may take. After a few innocuous questions posed by Dr. Halbsgut, I was somewhat taken aback when she abruptly ended the session. This unfortunate event was due to my having asked the doctor how to pronounce her last name. The only reason I inquired about the correct pronunciation of her name was motivated by belief that in order to have a foundation of mutual respect one should be able to address the other in a dignified and courteous manner. Unfortunately, Dr. Halbsgut took offense and ended the session. (I have included a copy of the email sent and my impression of the incident).

Shortly after the occurrence, I requested, first via my unit team, then subsequently, through email that I'm to be seen once again by the psychology department. The reply I received was most disconcerting. I was asked to explain my concerns in detail through electronic means before I would be allowed to be seen by psychology. Needless to say, I became increasingly concerned that, if I were to do as asked, the information provided could easily be compromised and shared with others.outside of the psychology department. Thereby, violating the doctor patient relationship of confidentiality.

I began to view the psychology department with suspicion which bordered on fear that there just might be a hidden agenda. After all of the interaction and history I had experienced, with various (BOP) psychology departments, from the time in the suicide watch area to my denial of admission into the Residential Drug Program (RDAP), by said department, as well as, having my application for suicide watch turned down by psychology, and now with the latest occurrence, I found myself filled with doubt, frustration, and a complete sense of helplessness. The only comfort and solace was to be found thousands of miles away in London, where my prospected fiancee, Shennell, who is a licensed psychoanalyst, resides.

Given these depressing and mentally burdening moments of despair, I was given yet another bit of emotionally troubling news. It seemed that the B.O.P. had decided to deny my fiance visitation rights at the prison where I'm currently confined, Butner FCI 2.

Here I start with the document, PS 5310.17, which is the "Psychology Services Manual" published by the Federal Bureau of Prisons.[7] The underlined words were underlined in the original statement. Because all the rules of law in the United States Constitution also govern the Federal Bureau of Prisons, I am making the point that the Eighth Amendment is relevant in the case of section 5310.17.

Co-author's note

This correlation between the Eighth Amendment and prisoner rights was echoed by a lawyer earlier on in this book. In searching the website for the United States Court of Appeals for the Armed Forces, one will find a document entitled: "First Principles: Constitutional Matters: Cruel and Unusual Punishment". Listed within it are a number of court cases with brief summaries. Included is the case, "United States, Appellee v. Claude F. White, Jr., Airman Basic; U.S. Air Force, Appellant", in which the summary reads: "(denial of adequate medical attention can constitute an Eighth Amendment or Article 55, UCMJ, violation; failure to provide basic psychiatric and mental health care can constitute deliberate indifference; however, an inmate is entitled to reasonable health care - it is not required that inmate health care be perfect or the best obtainable)."[8]

Clearly there is a common assumption of relevance across many platforms. Yet, the Psychology Services Manual that the U.S. Department of Justice puts out for the Federal Bureau of Prisons makes no mention of the Constitution or any of its amendments. But, indeed, prisoners are protected under the Eighth Amendment. As stated by Cornell Law School's Legal Information Institute: "Federal and state laws govern the establishment and administration of prisons as well as the rights of those who are incarcerated. Although prisoners do not have full constitutional rights, they are protected by the Eighth Amendment's prohibition against cruel and unusual punishment. This protection also requires that prisoners be afforded a minimum standard of living."

However, according to one Judicial Review:

> Courts tend to defer to prison officials regarding prisoners' rights. So long as the conditions or degree of a prisoner's confinement are within the sentence and not otherwise violative of the Constitution, the due process clause does not require judicial oversight. When prison regulations infringe on incarcerated individual's [sic] constitutional rights, the courts do not apply strict scrutiny. Rather, the rational basis test is used to determine whether the infringement may stand.[9]

It seems that Maurice and many other prisoners could attest to this latter fact. The situation he references here, with the psychologist at Butner, is just one example of the helpless and hopeless state that prisoners can enter into in this system. For reference, Jennifer Halbsgut received her Psy.D. in 2010. Her dissertation was titled "Masculine Gender Role Norms: Understanding the Conformity of Domestic Violence Perpetrators". She began working for the Bureau of Prisons in 2009 and, as of 2022, was still in their employment. Working at Butner at the time of Maurice's incarceration, she also participated in the prison's Doctoral Psychology Internship Program's Psychology Seminar Series in 2020. The topic was: "BOP Careers: An Overview and Q&A."[10]

In my 20 years of incarceration, I learned a lot about the many mental health professionals and programs connected to the prison system. Much of the time, it was with me being a patient. But I was also a "Suicide Watch Companion" – an institutional job I held at Hazelton. Psychology interns there trained us through the Suicide Watch Inmate Companion Program. Our job was to keep up constant observations on our brothers during these suicide watches.[11] I believe I was very useful in this role, and I wanted that position back when I got to Butner. But, as I reference in this essay, my application was denied.

I had also been previously denied admission to RDAP, the Residential Abuse Drug Program. It is a nine-month program where inmates are housed together separately from the other men. There we could get treatment, counseling, and resources of that nature. It just seemed like as hard as I was trying to help myself, and others inside, the psychology was trying just as hard to stop me.

As I mention in the essay, at this point I am really feeling like I can't win. But I had a little bit of hope in front of me because my fiancée, Shennel, was supposed to come visit me – all the way from England. We knew each other from way back but had subsequently made a strong connection online as I was researching mental health issues from prison. She became more and more interested in my story and even had me post a few things on her professional website. It felt really good to be heard by someone like her. Soon we became close.

I was really looking forward to her visit, only to learn that after all sorts of complicated paperwork she had to get through, they denied her visitation rights. (The details are explained more in Section III). It is hard to explain how devastating this kind of news can be when you are putting in all your hope, banking your positivity on seeing someone. When that doesn't happen, it feels personal, like the prison is laughing at you for having hope in the first place. And it just keeps happening.

Forward III: Hazelton 2012

FORWARD III

During a Thanksgiving holiday weekend in 2012 at the United States Penitentiary, Hazelton (USP), I was visited by my elder sisters, Tawana and Marquetta. It was during this visit that I was made aware of yet another example of the perpetual cycle of unprofessional and inexcusable' behavior by, the Bureau of Prisons (BOP) employee population.

As I sat before my sisters, Tawana, the youngest, who had never visited a prison before, appeared uneasy and somewhat insecure with the environment in which she found herself. In an attempt to break the ice and to ease the obvious tension that Tawana was exhibiting, I asked her an innocent question; "What took you two so long getting in here?"

The unexpected and shocking response came from Tawana. While Marquetta remained silent, Tawana, with bugged eyes dotting back and forth, raised her hands in defense as she spoke; her facial expression proposing a question of it's own. She explained to me the best she could that the officer stationed at the front entrance desk of the facility, not once, but twice denied her entry into visitation because he believed that she was not wearing clothing that was deemed appropriate or acceptable to BOP guidelines. She was told to either go and purchase new clothing or find a change of attire before she would be allowed entrance into the visiting area.

My sister Tawana, went on to tell me that no matter how much she attempted to reason with the officer and asking why the clothes she wore were deemed as too revealing, she was met with the same response. Realizing she had no other option but to go and purchase new clothing for her and her sister, who traveled from Washington D.C., she did so not knowing or thinking about bringing an extra change of clothes. Not once, but twice my sister Tawana was told yet again that the clothes she selected would deny her the privilege of visitation. Finally, on the third attempt, the officer permitted both of my sisters access to the visiting area.

My beloved sister, who has since passed away, Tawana's demeanor on that day was quite understandable. Both my other sister, Marquetta, and myself were humbled by my sister's strength of merit. Shortly after her visit with me, she passed away at the age of 42. Though on that autumn day in November, Tawana wore all of the tell-tale blemishes and badges of courage of her impending demise. Not only was her frail body riddled with purple cancerous lesions of Kaposi Sarcoma (KS), but Toxoplasmosis had begun to affect her motor skills. Cryptosporidiosis, a parasitical disease which consumes the digestive tract, and Cytomegalovirus, which. leads to blindness began to taking their affects. All of these diseases withered my sister down to just 85 pounds. Her physical appearance alone precluded my darling sister, who was always proud of her appearance, from displaying by her attire any indication of her fatal illness. It boggled both my sister and myself to comprehend how in the world this frail and extremely ill woman could be perceived as dressing provocatively.

It is quite reasonable to mention that, my sister Tawana, had to be escorted on this visit due to infirmity. She stated numerous times that she was bound and determined to see her brother before she died.

It was one of her last requests before the progressive and fatal stages of AIDS, which she had been bravely battling for the past few years, would end her life. And on that day of her visit, her symptoms were so pronounced that any reasonable person who possessed a shred of decency, sound mind, and vision would have taken notice.

Furthermore, I intended to take you on a personal journey which might allow you to have an increased ability to see beyond the immediate circumstances in this· text. To cast light upon a deeply embedded system of injustice and contradictory policies, which are continuously waged upon the prison population and their loved ones by the Federal Bureau of Prisons. The many injustices by numerous prisoners are being viewed as unilateral and often out of context.

Granted, I, myself, have in the past perpetrated societal injustices for which I am now paying the price for. In as much, when standing face to face with the universality of injustice, it can be painful, especially when we understand that all have a role in it. And although this is not meant to inspire guilt, or assign blame on the entirety of a system set in place to confine, correct, and transition the societal deviant of law, because this would also suggest that the implementation of a fair and humane structured system is useless or insignificant. However, it is to state that each of us, not merely the incarcerated, does indeed have a choice about whether we are going to strive to impede the behaviors that are systematically unjust, or support their existence simply by ignoring them. I contend that there shall be no neutral ground. To choose not to act against injustice is to opt for its continuance.

As I conclude, I pose yet another simple statement and question:

Though the agents of law are not responsible for the system which was created by others for their employment, should they nevertheless be held accountable for allowing, and at times encouraging creative methods which holds systematic injustice in place?

Maurice-W. Tyree

From the FCI-Hazelton Visitation Center website, updated August 2023:

> 9. APPROVED DRESS CODE - Visiting Attire:
> ALL visitors will be dressed in an appropriate manner and in good taste. Any visitor who arrives provocatively or inappropriately dressed will be denied the privilege of visiting. Inmates will inform visitors, prior to visiting, that clothing MUST be appropriate for an institution setting and should not demonstrate disrespect to others who may be present in the visiting room. All visitors must be fully attired, including shoes. Shoes must have a heel or be able to strap to the foot. Slipper type shoes, Shower Shoes or Flip-Flops are not permitted. Visitors are to refrain from wearing apparel which is revealing or suggestive. Visitors will refrain from wearing any clothing that contains sexually suggestive / offensive writing, or writing / logos that reference gangs. Shorts WILL NOT be permitted unless on a child under the age of 12. Dresses or skirts must be no shorter than knee-length, and may not have a slit above the knee. Any clothing that reveals any part of the buttocks or crotch area, sheer clothing, tank tops, halter tops, midriff tops,

strapless tops/dresses and spandex style clothing WILL NOT be permitted. Bib overalls and camouflage clothing WILL NOT be permitted. Undergarments containing metal (i.e. underwire bra) are not permitted. HOWEVER, UNDERGARMENTS ARE REQUIRED FOR ADMISSION. Only religious head wear may be worn. Visitors are not permitted to wear gray colored sweat wear, or any clothing khaki, orange, or green. Plain Tshirts in the following colors: Gray, Khaki, Green Orange, White, Red, or Yellow are NOT permitted. No medical scrubs or clothing resembling staff uniforms.
DENIAL OF VISITATION MUST BE AUTHORIZED BY THE COMPLEX WARDEN(USP/SPC) OR WARDEN (FCI).

My sisters were sent away three times on their scheduled visitation day before being able to see me. Is it really all that important what they were wearing? The sick fact is that the guards were able to look at my very sick sister and order her to leave the premises to purchase new clothing so she could visit her brother who was inside waiting for her. The complete loss of humanity in prison happens to everyone involved at some point. On both sides of the bars.[12]

Section III: Butner

SECTION III

5267.09   "Visiting   Regulation"   540.04/ Purpose and scope;

The Bureau of Prisons encourages visiting by family, friends, and community groups to maintain the morale of the inmate and to develop closer relationships between the inmate and family members or others in the community. The warden shall develop procedures consistent with this rule to permit inmate visiting.

The warden may restrict inmate visiting when necessary to ensure the security and good order of the institution.

<u>Page 54 of "Inmate Handbook", Inmate Rights and Responsibilities</u>

"you have the right to expect that as a human being you will be treated respectfully, impartially, and fairly by all personnel. You have the right to visit and correspond with members of your family, friends, and to correspond with members of the news media in keeping with Bureau rules and institution guidelines."

<u>Page 76-77 "Visitor Instructions"</u>

"Visitors at FCC Butner are encouraged to have visits in order to maintain family and community ties."

In my previous submission, I spoke of the failure of Mental Health Services, within the BOP, to provide substantial and meaningful care to myself, and that my only form of therapeutic counseling came from the woman

I intend to marry, who happens to be a licensed psychologist, in London England, which brings me to this next submission.

On account of her love, compassion, and training, she took it upon herself to send me appropriate self-help material, such as, "Cognitive Behavior Therapy" from the Center of Excellence (United Kingdom), and "The Tribes of The Person- Centred Nation: An introduction to the schools of therapy related to the person- centred approach" by Dr. Carl Rogers (United States), etc., which began to stem the floodwater of my despair. I slowly began to regain some semblance of humanity with all of it's shades of emotional well being. Nevertheless, I still felt betrayed, abandoned, and denied by the very people who are mandated to provide assistance in one's hour of need, who find themselves in the care custody and control of a careless entity. It was just another example of a Federal Bureaucracy's failure to do the correct thing.

It is a commentary on a system that leaves the individual with no other option but to fend for himself unless they are fortunate enough to have outside resources, and in my case, that being an ocean away.

Shennel, found herself equally frustrated and helpless, due to her professional training, which indicated to her, that I should be counseled personally, by a professional and not by electronic analysis. Little did I realize at that time, that Shennel's inability to see me personally, due to distance and scheduling conflicts, was to become another example in the compendium of the BOP's relentless march towards a problematic policy where the only solution is denied by a circumstance inherent in the problem, or by contradictory policies.

I first met Shennel Taylor, when both of our grandmothers were having a joint birthday party, in the U.S. years ago. Our relationship was originally innocent and platonic, but after re-establishing contact in the most unconventional way, via some personal literature I had a friend publish and post through social networking. Over time, with numerous pieces of correspondence and Trans-Atlantic phone calls, it began to evolve into a deep and abiding relationship, forged by mutual interests, empathy for each other, and within time, we both found ourselves longing for the same thing. Even though distance and physical barriers may separate us, the emotional attachment became a bond stronger than any geographical boundary and the only tangible obstacle standing in the way of our physical meeting was the United States Bureau of Prisons.

In April of 2016, Shennel made all of the arrangements, both scheduling and financial, in order so that she could travel to the United States, from London to North Carolina, for her purpose of visiting me, after initially having her visitation request form rejected once for not placing a return address on the posted envelope which contained the form.

Twice, for expressing on the form that she was of "Dual Race" opposed to just one of being "Black". Upon the third attempt, my counselor, Mr. Baskerville, assured me that he would have it approved as soon as he received it as the corrections would be made.

As Shennel boarded the plane at Heathrow, alongside her companion, Ms. Nattie Thornhill, who is also a citizen of Great Britain, and was approved on my visitation list on April 4, 2016, several weeks prior to their expected arrival, was operating under the impression that her visit had been approved by the BOP, or she would have never boarded the airplane.

After arriving in North Carolina, Shennel registered into the hotel she had previously reserved. Due to her late hour of arrival, she was unable to visit me until the following day. The next morning, after being informed by my counselor that Shennel Taylor was not approved on my visitation list and with no explanation forthcoming to me, I contacted Shennel to relay what I had been informed. With the heaviest of heart, and feeling completely dejected, Shennel was at a loss on how to best proceed. She decided that the best thing to do was to be pro-active and make some phone calls to Butner in the belief that some form of a simple clerical **error** had occurred. Within a few moments of making contact with staff at Butner (J. Baskerville and Unit Manager B. Hernandez), it became quite apparent to her that she was completely out of her area of expertise, and those to whom she spoke were completely without information and very obviously unconcerned, while viewing her concerns as an inconsequential and trivial dilemma. The information that they did provide was inconclusive and most puzzling. They stated that, Shennel Taylor, was not being allowed to visit because of a ''Red Flag'', which indicated some form of a criminal record.

Mr. Baskerville and Mr. Hernandez via conference call with Shennel, went on to further explain that they would not elaborate nor could they clarify or qualify the BOP's position. Shennel's only option, due to this revelation, and given the time frame and her limited schedule, was to go to the local Police Agency, in Cremount, North Carolina, in order to obtain a copy of any and all outstanding and/or all resolved criminal complaints or actions. Of course she knew beforehand what the background check would reveal, and indeed, once she obtained a National Crime Information Center background check, there was absolutely nothing to substantiate the BOP's claims of a "Red Flag' pertaining to any past, present, or pending criminal history.

Unfortunately, Shennel's efforts to clear her name were not accepted by staff members at Butner, who then gave another reason for their visiting refusal. They stated that her N.C.I.C. background check was invalid because it was done by a local state law enforcement agency, and not a federal law enforcement agency. And, even related documents that were forwarded from London to verify such non-history were rejected. Shennel, who was by now inconsolable and quite upset, had no'\ other alternative but to return to the United Kingdom without the comfort of seeing her prospective fiancee (Myself).

Upon returning home, and after making certain inquiries, Shennel was given the name of an attorney in the United States. Within days, she was in contact with Ms. Michelle Fields, Esq., and after paying a substantial retainer fee of $1500.00, she engaged said attorney, in the hopes of resolving what appeared to her as a simple misunderstanding.

After an exhaustive background check by Ms. Fields' private investigator and with numerous requests to the FBI, for freedom and information documents pertaining to and all criminal history, what had been known all along by both Shennel and myself was confirmed. Simply put, that at no time in the past or at present moment, whether in the United States, or elsewhere on the entire planet Earth, has Shennel Taylor ever been convicted for any criminal activity.

Furthermore, it should be noted that Ms. Shennel Taylor is a licensed psychologist in the United Kingdom, as well as, a partner in business in London England. Also, Shennel has volunteered her time to a variety of Non-Government Organizations (N.G.O.), while at the same time donating monies to non-profit charitable funds, and is considered to be a most respected and generous person within her community. The mere idea that Ms. Taylor has done anything of a felonious nature is not only a slight on her unblemished character, but is at the same time a scurrilous attempt to link my criminal history to her, by impugning her impeccable credentials. An act which is not only psychologically injurious to Ms. Taylor, as well as myself, and those intimately involved with this emotional bureaucratic roller coaster.

The continuing efforts of the BOP to deprive Shennel and myself of the nurturing comfort of visitation, is in direct conflict with the United States Bureau of Prisons' own policy, a policy which strongly encourages family and friends to visit the incarcerated. Thus, affording both the chance to strengthen relationships and ties with the outside community.

It is also viewed by the BOP, as a way to ensure the psychological well being, while lessening potential discipline problems among the incarcerated.

It was well noted and stated by Lee Petro, esq., the Washington attorney who represented inmates' families before the FCC, in the fight against prison phone pricing, which prison officials sought to ban the privileges of contact visitation altogether; "Every study done on prison visitation, shows that even a single visit can have a major impact of limiting recidivism. If your job as a prison official is to stop people from coming back, why would you ban one of the most effective ways to put people on a better path, then turn around and use the money to pay for new programs that may, or may not work? This defies logic."

It has now been almost a year and a half since Shennel's denial to visit me at Butner FCI 2. During this period of time, an exorbitant amount of money has been expended. Many hours of effort, by many parties has been invested in order for this emotionally draining and mindlessly motivated visitation refusal to get resolved. Over the past year and a half, Shennel has traveled to the United States without hinderance by U.S. customs officials, or any other federal or state agency, leaving her with the stark realization that until this "Catch-22" nightmare ends, she will be unable to see and visit with the man she has chosen never to abandon.

To date, the BOP has yet once again changed it's position, and is now contending that indeed, Ms. Shennel Taylor's character is without blemish, and that she has no, and I repeat, no criminal record. Unfortunately, the BOP has now declared and decided, that Ms. Taylor will still not be allowed visitation privileges with me, because the relationship with which we both treasure, began after my incarceration. Therefore, it is not a valid relationship. The credibility of a relationship has now become the narrative behind the BOP's refusal. A narrative which once again puts the burden of proof upon the innocent, who ask for nothing more than that which is rightfully due to countless numbers of those incacerated in the Federal Bureau of Prisons.

Co-author's note

The legal case led by Lee Petro, as mentioned in this section of the essay, culminated in the Martha Wright-Reed Just and Reasonable Communications Act. It was signed into law in January 2023. This was part of a larger 'phone justice' movement by advocates of prison reform. This Act essentially clarified the Federal Communications Commission's (FCC) ability to regulate phone and video calls from inside of prisons. These calls can cost exorbitant sums in some institutions; the goal being to cap those prices across the board. Activists argue that the data shows the major importance of contact with loved ones for the betterment of mental health in prisoners, yet quite often it is impossible for inmates to cover the cost of a phone or video call to family or friends.[13]

Conclusion

CONCLUSION

It is very easy to find fault within the United States' Federal Prison system, for there are many faults to be found. However, the most obvious and inexcusable are, a failure to start dialogue where concerns and inadequacies can be addressed, to find efficient solutions in a circumstantial and humanistic manner for the health of the ever evolving society depends on such a process.

The first step to be taken must come from the community. One where an independent and non-political investigative committee would be empowered to explore and compare data concerning actual applications of services within the BOP, as opposed to the purported and documented reports given by the prison's administration.

This community committee should be comprised from across sections of society which may include, but not limited to, clergymen and women from various ideologies, civic leaders from a variety of non-governmental organizations, educators with an academic background in contemporary penological studies. It should also include; formerly incarcerated individuals, along with families who have loved ones incarcerated.

This investigation committee must have access to all real time and public information, from both those presently incarcerated, and the administration who *is* in charge of compiling all data within the federal prisons. Without complete disclosure and cooperation, the committee will be unable to reach a realistic evaluation, or form any kind of representational conclusion.

For far too long, the United States prison system has been allowed to operate in a vacuum completely void of accountability, oversight, and criticism. Decade after decade the United States prison system has been given a license to experiment with the quality of care and life given to those incarcerated, which has resulted in a more draconian application concerning the expansion of denial of basic humanitarian services, and an almost cataractic vision towards promoting programs that decrease recidivism and morale, while at the same time embracing counter-productive philosophies towards rehabilitation.

No longer can we as a society look upon those incarcerated as unsalvageable outsweepings to be cast upon the wretched waste pile of forgotten humanity.

This community committee must be empowered to impose federal legislation, which will address the many inequities and administrative failures by the Bureau of Prisons. This committee should also be empowered to call before it's hearing any and all parties, documents, or relevant information it deems applicable to its ongoing proceedings. No governmental agency, or related records should be exempt from this investigation, for they are not protected under the National Security Clause or Executive Privilege. Without these powers, the panel will find itself stymied and hobbled, without any form of a mandate to arrive at a constructive and mutually beneficial resolution.

With the above in mind, our society no longer has the luxury to turn a blind eye to the way it warehouses and destroys the lives of millions of its own citizens. Many, such as my disproportionate social group, have done nothing more than to transgress against ill-conceived and failed drug policies, pertaining to "The War On Drugs".

The following are a list of some of the conditions which give rise to mental and/or emotional traumas that justify the diagnosis of PTSD:

--- A serious threat or harm to one's life or physical integrity.
--- A threat or harm to one's children, spouse or close relative.
--- Sudden destruction of one's house or community.
--- Seeing another person injured or killed as a result of an accident or physical violence.
--- Learning about a serious threat to a relative or a close friend being kidnapped, tortured or killed.
--- Stressor is experienced with intense fear, terror and helplessness.
--- Stressor and disorder is considered to be more serious and will last longer when the stressor is of human design.

It is important to note that the manual states that any one of the above stressors is enough to cause PTSD.

Today, those who are diagnosed with PTSD exhibit symptoms that may require clinical treatment inclusive of drug therapy. Some of the symptoms of PTSD include;

--- Intense psychological distress at exposure to internal or external cues that symbolize an aspect of the traumatic event.
--- Physiological reactivity on exposure to internal or external cues.
--- Marked diminished interest or participation in significant activities.
--- Feeling of detachment or estrangement from others.

Restricted range of affect.

Sense of foreshortened future (does not expect to have a career, marriage, children or normal life span.

--- Difficulty falling or staying asleep,
--- Irritability or outbursts of anger.
--- Difficulty concentrating.

Remember, these are just some of the symptoms that an individual may exhibit having had direct or indirect exposure to a single traumatic event.

What about those who experienced a lifetime, in and out of bondage? For I have, with very little pause in my life span, been exposed to all the 16 aforementioned, as well as others.

And finally, a most prophetic scriptural verse which states;

"You have sown the wind, now you will reap the whirlwind."

If the Bureau of Prisons continues to travel down the same path, and consciously choose not to alter their present course of ineptness, indifference, and discriminatory hazards, then the whirlwind they have created will surely consume us all.

I humbly beg your pardon, I ask for your help to aid in an arbitrary capacity, and preserve health within the bowel of American society and the remorseful minds which lie in its thorn.

Sincerely Submitted,
Maurice W. Tyree

[Appendix missing from essay]

Co-author's note

While there have been several government coalitions created to address prison reform in this country, such as within the federal Committee on Oversight and Accountability, there have been fewer 'citizens' committees as proposed by Maurice here. He is not alone in his thinking on this matter either. According to a report by the Council on Criminal Justice:

> Research supports the proposition that oversight boards with authority, independence, and the ability to conduct random inspections can produce positive results. Such boards should be trained and should establish measurable goals that can be easily evaluated. They should play an advisory role, rather than possessing operational authority, but should be equipped with the power to obtain data, analyze it, and distribute findings to the public.[14]

Some states are convening such committees. In Arizona, in 2023, an executive order was issued by the governor to establish a commission:

> …appointed by the governor and will include members of the Arizona Senate and House of Representatives, a representative of an "inmate advocacy organization," a member with a background in rehabilitative programming for prisoners, two people formerly incarcerated in Arizona prisons, members with medical and mental health care experience, a family member of a recently incarcerated person, and a representative of correctional workers.[15]

While it may seem as if prison reform makes for strange bedfellows – Arizona not being the first state one might imagine as interested in such progressive reform – sometimes these moves are simply thinly veiled law and order-type initiatives. In December 2018, then-President Trump signed into law the First Step Act. It was touted as "a bi-partisan effort to improve criminal justice outcomes, as well as to reduce the size of the federal prison population while also creating mechanisms to maintain public safety." The attorney general was then tasked with consulting an Independent Review Committee. Chosen as the 'independent, non-partisan' consultant for that committee was the 70-year-old Hudson Institute, a conservative think tank out of Washington, D.C. While the Act has had some success, by decreasing harsh sentences for non-violent crimes, the Bureau of Prisons continues to resist the transparency needed for clear assessment of the efficacy of some of the programs implemented. It is, as they say, a work in progress.[16]

In his essay, Maurice foresees the loopholes the BOP might take in order to block access to these committees of relevant information. He makes mention of the National Security [Act], for example, which provides that: "This authority may be used for any acquisition when disclosure of the Government's needs would compromise the national security (*e.g.,* would violate security requirements); it shall not be used merely because the acquisition is classified, or merely because access to classified matter will be necessary to submit a proposal or to perform the contract."[17] And perhaps, Maurice posits, a president may even choose to invoke 'Executive Privilege' in an attempt to block access to certain prison records. This may seem like paranoia to some but, for anyone who has experience with, around, and inside the prison system, their experience is often that conspiracies are more the norm than the exception.

This essay can be seen as a plea to anyone who will listen. It is an appeal for understanding that humans live behind these bars, inside these prison walls. After reading Maurice's story, perhaps this becomes more apparent to the reader – the fact that the untenable conditions inside a multitude of penal institutions are affecting other humans' fathers, mothers, sisters, brothers, cousins, teachers, friends, and lovers. The alleged mission of the contemporary prison system is rehabilitation. Yet, placing people in cages, surveilling their every move, lying, cheating, and gaslighting them on a regular basis, cannot possibly allow for rehabilitation except in the most exceptional of cases. Like that of Maurice.

But this is not a pull-yourself-up-by-your-bootstraps Cinderella story. More it is a there-are-no-bootstraps-in-prison story. Fortunately, there are many previously incarcerated people like Maurice who have become activists and reformists. And there is a plethora of information to be had on the subject via literature, podcasts, and community talks, among other sources. There are also, of course, the prisons themselves that often provide opportunity for visitors and volunteers to gain insight through various activities and programs.

There is a groundswell of people who feel that it is imperative to change this system drastically, for the sake of *all* humanity. The authors of this book hope that the reader becomes moved to join this particular movement, in whatever capacity they might see fit. At the least, it is hoped that the reader will, after spending so much time among the words of Mr. Tyree, consider those who are presently imprisoned as brother and sister – 'one of us' instead of other.

Recommended projects

1. Choose one of the following prison reform organizations. (Or choose one, that you might be familiar with, or that is local). Write a summary of their mission and provide one specific 'success' featured in their materials. Afterwards, consider following that chosen organization on social media or subscribing to their newsletter.

    More Than Our Crimes https://morethanourcrimes.org/
    The Sentencing Project https://www.sentencingproject.org/
    Innocence Project https://innocenceproject.org/our-work/
    Equal Justice Initiative https://eji.org/bryan-stevenson/
    Vera Institute of Justice https://www.vera.org/

2. Screen and then review one of the following films. Consider how similar or different the presentation of prison life is as compared to that told in this book.
    Cool Hand Luke
    Escape from Alcatraz
    Brubaker
    The Shawshank Redemption
    Dead Man Walking
    Black August

3. Choose one of the books referenced by the author in this memoir. (Or see Recommended further reading page). Read

it and then write a book review, considering any similarities or differences you see between this book and the one you have chosen. Why do you think Mr. Tyree might have found that particular book interesting?

Notes

Introduction: Letter to the court

1. Yusef Salaam, "Born on purpose, with a purpose," in *Better, Not Bitter: Living on Purpose in The Pursuit of Racial Justice* (New York, NY: Grand Central Publishing) 2021. p. 15.
2. M. Fritz, and C.Booker, *How a criminal justice reporter built trust with prisoners to highlight conditions inside*, Public Broadcasting Service.
3. Ta-Nehisi Coates, *Between the world and me* (UK: Text Publishing Company) 2015. p. 48
4. George Jackson, and J. Jackson, *Soledad brother: the prison letters of George Jackson* (Chicago: Lawrence Hill Books) 2006. pp. 261-262.

Chapter 1: Fending for myself

1. "Dick Gregory - family values," *Maarifa Circle,* YouTube, June 16, 2016.
2. Juleyka Lantigua-Williams, "Ava DuVernay's 13th reframes American history, *The Atlantic,* October 6, 2016.
3. One obstacle to these communications has been the exorbitant fees attached to phone calls in prison. There is a movement to reduce these rates. This issue is discussed in greater detail in chapter six. See also "California's free prison calls are repairing estranged relationships and aiding rehabilitation" by Kwasi Gyamfi Asiedu and Helen Li, *Los Angeles Times,* July 27, 2023.
4. Demetrius Buckley, "The powerlessness of parenting from prison," *Life Inside,* The Marshall Project. March 11, 2022.

5. Ryan Moser, "Between addiction and prison, I left my boy to grow up without a Dad," *Life Inside,* The Marshall Project, Nov. 18, 2022.

Chapter 2: No more keeping it to myself

1. Lorraine Adams, "A breach in guards' invincibility," *The Washington Post,* Sept. 2, 1996.
2. Pam Bailey, "FCI Hazelton: called 'misery mountain' for a reason," *More Than Our Crimes,* Sep. 5, 2022.
3. Michael Balsamo, "'Inmates can lose their lives quickly here': what to know about the West Virginia prison where 'Whitey' Bulger was killed," *Boston Globe,* Nov. 1, 2018.

Chapter 3: Sankofa

1. David Murphey and P. Mae Cooper, "Parents behind bars: what happens to their children?" *Child Trends*, Oct. 2015.
2. Precious Skinner-Osei and Dhiny Mercedes, "Collateral consequences: the impact of incarceration on African American fathers and their sons," *Journal of Forensic Social Work* 7 (1):1-13, Jan 3, 2023.

Chapter 4: Cousins, comrades, cellies, friends, and teachers

1. Eilene Zimmerman, "What makes some people more resilient than others," *The New York Times.* June 18, 2020.
2. "Russell Conwell explains why diamonds are a man's best friend," *History Matters.*
3. "How blacks and whites die differently in prison," *The Marshall Project,* 12/15/2016, accessed 6/28/2023
4. "Suicides increasing in California prisons," *Equal Justice Initiative,* 10/04/19, accessed 6/28/2023.
5. Susan Nembhard and Natalie Lima, "To improve safety, understanding and addressing the link between childhood trauma and crime is key," *Urban Wire,* Urban Institute, August 9, 2022.
6. Carol Craty, "Obama administration proceeds with controversial prison purchase," *CNN Politics,* 10/02/2012.

7. Pam Bailey, "Medical malpractice in prison: where is the care?" *More Than Our Crimes*, March 4, 20

8. Christina Pazzanese, "Supreme court may halt health care guarantees for inmates," *The Harvard Gazette*, March 2, 2023.

Chapter 5: Letter of resignation

1. This is attributed to Dr. Welsing by the late South African activist Robert Sobukwe on his archived Tumblr page. No confirmation of this attribution has been accessed as of this date.

2. Frances Cress Welsing, *The Isis (Yssis) papers*, 1st ed (Chicago: Third World Press 1991) (10).

3. Edward D. Sargent, "Controversial Black doctor provokes reporters' reactions," *The Washington Post*. September 25, 1980.

Chapter 6: "Mental health's undocumented and oppressive continuum"

1. Leary, Joy DeGruy. *Post traumatic slave syndrome: America's legacy of enduring injury and healing*. Milwaukie, Oregon: Uptone Press, 2005 (29).

2. Liz Benecchi, "Recidivism imprisons American progress," *Harvard Political Review*, August 8, 2021.

3. "Martin Luther King, 'I have a dream' 28 August 1963," *Human Rights Library*, University of Minnesota.

4. Barack Obama, "Remarks by the president at the NAACP conference," *The White House: Office of the Press Secretary*, July 14, 2015.

5. "Violent crime control and law enforcement act of 1994—conference report," *Government Printing Office*, Volume 140, Number 122 (Tuesday, August 23, 1994).

6. Allison Graves, "Did Hillary Clinton call African-American youth 'superpredators?'" *Politifact*, The Poynter Institute, August 28, 2016.

7. "Psychology services manual," *U.S. Department of Justice; Federal Bureau of Prisons*, Program statement Opi Rsd/Psb Number P5310.17. August 25, 2016. Accessed 10/6/23, PDF

8. "First principles: constitutional matters: cruel and unusual punishment," *United States Court of Appeals for the Armed Forces,* 2001.
9. "Prisoners' rights," *Legal Information Institute,* Cornell Law School, April 27, 2023.
10. "Psychology doctoral internship," *Federal correctional complex Butner, North Carolina,* Dept. of Justice, 2024- 2025.
11. According to a 2005 study, "Prison suicide watches done by other inmates, instead of prison staff, reduce the frequency and duration of watches, benefit inmate observers and reduce costs, according to a study conducted by Federal Bureau of Prisons." See, "Suicide Watches by inmates benefit all," *Monitor on Psychology,* June 2005, Vol 36, No. 7 htps://www.apa.org/monitor/jun05/suicide.html.
12. In September 2023, a group of senators wrote a letter to Attorney General Garland regarding corroborated reports of specific illegal activities by staff at FCC Hazelton. The infractions included multiple coverups of racial slurs; destruction of prisoner property; and violent assault against prisoners. They conclude the letter by demanding that the Dept. of Justice and Bureau of Prisons provide related information to them promptly. See "Durbin, Grassley, Manchin, Capito Call on DOJ & BOP to Investigate Reports of Abusive Treatment at FCC Hazelton," *US Senate on the Judiciary,* Sept. 12, 2023. htps://www.judiciary.senate.gov/press/releases/durbin- grassley-manchin-capito-call-on-doj-and-bop-to-investigate-reports-of-abusive-treatment-at-fcc-hazelton
13. "Since you asked: what's next for prison and jail phone justice now that the Martha Wright-Reed just and reasonable communications act is law?" *Prison Policy Initiative.* See also, "Inflation! even pennies count in prison," *Voices Unlocked,* More Than Our Crimes, Sept. 26, 2023. https://www.audacy.com/podcast/voices-unlocked-3d4b5/episodes/inflation-even-pennies-count-in-prison-b5623

14. "Federal priorities task force report - 8 - establish oversight of the bureau of prisons," *Council on Criminal Justice,* n.d. Accessed 10/16/23.

15. Jimmy Jenkins and Stacey Barchenger, "Reformers applaud Hobbs' plans for an oversight commission for troubled Arizona prisons," *The Arizona Republic,* January 26, 2023.

16. See, "What is the first step act — and what's happening with it?" *Brennan Center for Justice,* 6/23/20 and "An overview of the first step act," *Federal Bureau of Prisons,* accessed 10/16/2023.

17. "6.302-6 National security," *Federal acquisition regulation,* United States Government. | Sept. 22, 2023. Accessed 10/16/2023. https://www.acquisition.gov/far/6.302-6.

References

13th. Directed by Ava DuVernay, *Kandoo Films*, October 7, 2016.

Adams, L. (1996). A Breach in guards' invincibility. *The Washington Post*, [online]. Available at: www.washingtonpost.com/archive/politics/1996/09/02/a-breach-in-guards- invincibility/d0f9c4cc-4562-482f-9aac-fb9be699d003/#comments. [Accessed 15 Dec. 22].

Bailey, P. (2022). FCI Hazelton: called 'Misery Mountain' for a reason. *More Than Our Crimes*, [online]. Available at: https://morethanourcrimes.org/voices/fci-hazelton-cauldron-of- misery/ [Accessed 21 July 2023].

——— (2023). "Medical malpractice in prison: where is the care?" *More Than Our Crimes*. https://morethanourcrimes.org/voices/medical-malpractice-in-prison-where-is- the-care/ [Accessed 14 August 2023].

Balsamo, M. (2018). 'Inmates can lose their lives quickly here': what to know about the West Virginia prison where 'Whitey' Bulger Was Killed. *Boston Globe*, [online]. Available at: www.boston.com/news/national-news/2018/11/01/whitey-bulger-usp-hazelton/ [Accessed 21 July 2023].

Benecchi, L. (2021). Recidivism imprisons American progress. *Harvard Political Review*, [online]. Available at: https://harvardpolitics.com/recidivism-american- progress/ [Accessed 4 Oct. 2023].

Buckley, D. (2022). The Powerlessness of parenting from prison. *Life Inside*. The Marshall Project. https://www.themarshallproject.org/2022/03/11/the-powerlessness-of- parenting-from-prison [Accessed 23 July 2023].

Coates, Ta-Nehisi. (2015). *Between the world and me*. UK: Text Publishing Company.

Council on Criminal Justice. *Federal priorities task force report - 8 - establish oversight of the Bureau of Prisons*, [online]. Available at: https://counciloncj.foleon.com/taskforce/federal-priorities/rec8/ [Accessed 16 Oct. 2023].

Cratty, Carol. (2012). Obama administration proceeds with controversial prison purchase. *Politics*, [online]. Available at: https://www.cnn.com/2012/10/02/politics/illinois-prison/index.html [Accessed 14 August 2023].

Equal Justice Initiative. (2019). *Suicides increasing in California prisons despite decades of reform efforts*. [online]. Available at: https://eji.org/news/suicides-increasing-in-california- prisons/#:~:text=There%20were%20448%20total%20suicides,continue%20to%20rise%20i n%202019. [Accessed 5 Dec. 2023].

Federal acquisition regulation. (2023). 6.302-6 National security. United States government, [online]. Available at: www.acquisition.gov/far/6.302-6 [Accessed 16 Oct. 2023].

Frankl V. E. (1984). *Man's search for meaning: an introduction to logotherapy*. 3rd ed. New York: Simon & Schuster.

Fritz, M., Booker, C. (2022). *How a criminal justice reporter built trust with prisoners to highlight conditions inside*. Public Broadcasting Service, [online]. Available at: www.pbs.org/newshour/show/how-a-criminal-justice-reporter-built-trust-with-prisoners-to-highlight-conditions-inside [Accessed 22 Nov. 2022].

Government Printing Office. (1994). *Violent crime control and law enforcement act of 1994— Conference Report.* [Online]. Volume 140, Number 122. www.govinfo.gov/content/pkg/CREC-1994-08-23/html/CREC-1994-08-23-pt1- PgS16.htm [Accessed 11 Sept. 2023].

Graves, A. (2016). Did Hillary Clinton call African-American youth 'superpredators?' *Politifact*. The Poynter Institute, [online]. Available at: www.politifact.com/factchecks/2016/aug/28/reince-priebus/did-hillary-clinton- call-african-american-youth-su/ [Accessed 11 Sept. 23].

Gregory, D. (2016). - *Family values.* [*YouTube*] Available at: www.youtube.com/watch?v=z9rnrqD3UzYn [Accessed 29 July 2023].

Jackson, G. and Jackson, J. (2006). *Soledad brother: the prison letters of George Jackson.* Chicago: Lawrence Hill Books.

Jenkins, J., Barchenger, S. (2023). Reformers applaud Hobbs' plans for an oversight commission for troubled Arizona prisons. *The Arizona Republic,* [online]. Available at: www.azcentral.com/story/news/local/arizona-breaking/2023/01/25/arizona-prison- oversight-commission-created-by-governor-katie-hobbs/69841037007/ [Accessed 16 Oct. 2023].

Lantigua-Williams, J. (2016). Ava DuVernay's 13th reframes American history. *The Atlantic,* [online]. Available at: www.theatlantic.com/entertainment/archive/2016/10/ava-duvernay-13th- netflix/503075/ [Accessed 23 July 2023].

Leary, J.D. (2005). *Post traumatic slave syndrome: America's legacy of enduring injury and healing.* Milwaukie, Oregon: Uptone Press, PDF. Available at: https://coalchicago.com/Images/2021/09/Post-Traumatic-Slave-Syndrome-Americas-Legacy-of-Enduring-Injury-and- Healing-by-Joy-DeGruy-1.pdf [Accessed 3 Oct. 2023].

Lopez, G. (2020). The controversial 1994 crime law that Joe Biden helped write, explained. *Vox Media,* [online]. Available at: www.vox.com/policy-and-politics/2019/6/20/18677998/joe-biden-1994-crime-bill-law-mass-incarceration [Accessed 11 Sept. 2023].

King, Martin Luther. "I Have a Dream." Human Rights Library. University of Minnesota. 28 August 1963. http://hrlibrary.umn.edu/education/lutherspeech.html [Accessed 4 Sept. 2023]

The Marshall Project. (2016). *How Blacks and whites die differently in prison.* [Online]. Available at: www.themarshallproject.org/2016/12/15/how-blacks-and-whites-die-differently-in-prison [Accessed 28 June 2023].

Moser, R. (2022). Between addiction and prison, I left my boy to grow up without a dad. *Life Inside*, [online]. The Marshall Project. Available at: https://www.themarshallproject.org/2022/11/18/between-addiction-and-prison-i-left-my-boy-to-grow-up-without-a-dad [Accessed 23 July 2023].

Murphey, D. and Cooper. P. (2015). Parents behind bars: what happens to their children? *Child Trends*, [online]. Available at: www.childtrends.org/wp- content/uploads/2015/10/2015-42ParentsBehindBars.pdf [Accessed 9 March 2023].

Nembhard, S. and Lima, N. (2022). To improve safety, understanding and addressing the link between childhood trauma and crime is key. *Urban Wire*, [online]. Urban Institute. Available at: www.urban.org/urban-wire/improve-safety-understanding-and-addressing-link- between-childhood-trauma-and-crime-key

Obama, B. (2015). Remarks by the president at the NAACP conference. *The White House: Office of the Press Secretary*, [online]. Available at: https://obamawhitehouse.archives.gov/the-press-office/2015/07/14/remarks-president-naacp-conference [Accessed 8 Sept, 2023].

Pazzanese, C. (2023). Supreme court may halt health care guarantees for inmates. *The Harvard Gazette*, [online]. Available at: https://news.harvard.edu/gazette/story/2023/03/supreme-court-may-halt-health-care- guarantees-for-inmates/ [Accessed 14 Aug. 2023].

"Prisoners' rights." *Legal Information Institute*. (2023). Cornell Law School. https://www.law.cornell.edu/wex/prisoners%27_rights#:~:text=Federal%20and%20state%20laws%20govern,against%20cruel%20and%20unusual%20punishment. [Accessed 12 Oct. 2023].

Prison Policy Initiative. (2023). *Since you asked: what's next for prison and jail phone justice now that the Martha Wright-Reed just and reasonable communications act is law?*[Online]. Available at: www.prisonpolicy.org/blog/2023/01/19/martha-wright-reed-act/. [Accessed 13 Oct. 2023].

"Psychology doctoral internship." (2024-2025). *Federal Correctional Complex Butner, North Carolina*. Dept. of Justice. www.Bop.Gov/Jobs/Docs/Bux_Internship_Brochure.Pdf. [Accessed 12 Oct. 2023].

"Psychology services manual." (2016). *U.S. Department of Justice; Federal Bureau of Prisons*. Program Statement Opi Rsd/Psb Number P5310.17. [Online]. Available at: www.bop.gov/policy/progstat/531 0_017.pdf [Accessed 6 Oct. 23].

"Russell Conwell explains why diamonds are a man's best friend." *History Matters*. https://historymatters.gmu.edu/d/5769/ [Accessed 30 May 2023].

Salaam, Y. (2021). *Better, not bitter: living on purpose in the pursuit of racial justice*. New York, NY: Grand Central Publishing.

Sargent, E. D. (1980). Controversial Black doctor provokes reporters' reactions. *The Washington Post*, [online]. Available at: https://www.washingtonpost.com/archive/local/1980/09/25/controversial-black-doctor- provokes-reporters-reactions/fb5487f4-a45d-49d6-a235-b69d13d42ff0/ [Accessed 28 Sept 23].

Skinner-Osei, P., Mercedes, D. (2023). Collateral consequences: the impact of incarceration on african american fathers and their sons. *Journal of Forensic Social Work* 7 (1):1-13. https://doi.org/10.15763/issn.1936-9298.2023.7.1.1-13. [Accessed 6 March 23].

Sobukwe, R. Africa for Africans. *Tumblr*, [online]. Available at: https://nevermindreal.tumblr.com/post/134520546091 [Accessed 28 Sept. 2023].

United States Court of Appeals for the Armed Forces. (2001). First principles: *constitutional matters: cruel and unusual punishment*, [online]. Available at: www.Armfor.Uscourts.Gov/Digest/IB4.Htm#:~:Text=(Denial%20of%20adequat e%20medical%20attention,Health%20care%20be%20perfect%20or [Accessed 12 Oct. 2023].

Welsing F. C. 1991.*The Isis (Yssis) papers*. 1st ed. Chicago: Third World Press. https://ia801008.us.archive.org/ 29/items/TheIsisPapersFrancisCressWelsing/the_isis_papers_-_francis_cress_welsing%20%281%29.pdf [Accessed 11 Sept. 2023].

Zimmerman, E. (2020). What makes some people more resilient than others. *The New York Times*, [online]. Available at: https://www.nytimes.com/2020/06/18/health/resilience-relationships- trauma .html#:~:text=Southwick%20says%20resilient%20people%20 reappraise,system% 2C%20and%20they%20support%20others. [Accessed 23 Oct. 2023].

Recommended further reading

13th. (2016). *Kandoo Films*. DuVernay, Ava.

Coates, Ta-Nehisi. (2015). *Between the world and me*. UK: Text Publishing Company.

Jackson, G. and Jackson, J. (1994). *Soledad brother: the prison letters of George Jackson*. Chicago: Lawrence Hill Books.

Salaam, Y. (2021). *Better, not bitter: living on purpose in the pursuit of racial justice*. New York, NY: Grand Central Publishing.

X, Malcolm. (1992). *The autobiography of Malcolm X*. Bantam Doubleday Dell Publishing Group

Index

administrative remedies, ineffectiveness of 243

Adverse Childhood Experiences (ACEs) 219

aging 29, 32, 33

ancestors 112, 189, 200, 250, 258, 273

ancestral patterns 111

Arizona 321

Avis 177

Bailey, Pam 242

Better, Not Bitter: Living on Purpose in the Pursuit of Racial Justice (Salaam) 12

Between the World and Me (Coates) 17

Biden, Joe 287, 288

Black dreams 221

Black Oath, A 253

Blakinger, Keri 14

bondage 262, 263, 270, 319

Bradshaw, Miss 271, 272

Brandt, Judge 10, 18, 25

Buckley, Demetrius 52

Bureau of Prisons (BOP) 5, 6, 19, 21, 180, 227, 261, 264, 267, 271, 292, 295, 296, 297, 298, 302, 304, 308, 312, 314, 317, 320, 322

California, penal system of 208

changing mind 55

childhood abuse and neglect, impact of 219

Christianity 74, 76, 78, 109

Clinton, Bill 287, 289

Clinton, Hilary 288

Coates, Ta-Nehisi 17

Coles-El, George "Mesro" 209

consciousness 165, 184, 193

conversion effort, of Maurice 16

Conwell, Russell 188, 190, 193

Council on Criminal Justice 321

court, letter to 1–9

COVID pandemic 56

Cress Theory on Color Confrontation 256, 257

deep discussion 170

DeGruy, Joy A. 47, 262, 269

Deitch, Michele 208

Demetrius 52, 141, 142, 144, 145, 151; letters to 144–45, 151–52

desperation 103, 242

DuVernay, Ava 46–47

education, of Maurice 3, 4, 5, 14, 17, 18

Eighth Amendment 243, 290, 295, 296

Eric 161, 163, 165, 168, 194, 234; letters to 163–67

Evolutionist 195, 198, 199

family connection, as motivation 97

family theme 63

father of Maurice, death of 8, 14, 82–85

FCI-Hazelton Visitation Center 303

Fear of a Black planet (album) 257

Federal Committee on Oversight and Accountability 320

Federal Communications Commission 314

Federal Correctional Institution (FCI) Butner Medium II 15, 266

Fields, Anthony 60

First Step Act 321

forgiveness 139, 169

Frankl, Viktor 6, 184

freedom 6, 17, 58, 89, 90, 91, 93, 94, 127, 183, 190, 197, 200, 251, 258, 27, 278, 311

Gandhi, M. K., Mahatma 78

Gregory, Dick 46, 180

Halbsgut, Jennifer 293, 296

hard work 168

Harvard Gazette, The 242

heart disease 88, 242

Hernandez, Aaron 228, 229

heroin addiction 4, 8, 13, 240

history, knowing 123

Hoffman, Kenneth 60, 61

Holder, Eric 234

homosexuality, Maurice's stance on 176

Hoover, Herbert 132, 289

Imani, letters to 107–9, 120–22

Inside-Out Prison Exchange Program 14, 224, 227

instincts 107, 109, 168

Isis Papers, The (Welsing) 255

Islam 72, 75, 76, 77, 159, 162, 163

isolation 14, 32, 38, 46, 57, 58, 59, 84, 86, 209, 289, 291, 292

Jackson, George 20, 21, 39, 61, 169, 172, 198

Kennedy, Anthony 208
King, Martin Luther, Jr. 58, 77, 78, 258, 276, 283
Kirby, Jeri 227; letters to 230–33, 235–36, 238–40, 243–47

Lakeisha 41, 44, 48, 55
Lakeisha, letter to and from 41–44
Le'mia 39, 51, 83, 105, 107, 111, 115, 116, 119, 122, 123, 125, 137, 138, 139, 146, 150; letters to 105–7, 111–14, 116–19, 123–37, 146–50
Leary, Joy DeGruy 269
loneliness 37, 58, 102, 103
love 29, 35, 37, 38, 39, 40, 43, 45, 48, 50, 62, 63, 64, 65, 66, 67, 68, 69, 74, 83, 89, 90, 92, 93, 96, 105, 106, 107, 112, 113, 118, 121, 122, 132, 140, 145, 146, 150, 169, 207, 306

Maaj. *see* Noah (aka Maaj)
Mafuz, letter to 187–92
Man's Search for Meaning (Frankl) 184
Marquetta, letters to 27–31, 48–50, 53–55, 61–63, 64–66, 78–83, 86–88, 95–99
Marshall Project, The 52, 207, 208
Martha Wright-Reed Just and Reasonable Communications Act 314

Maurice 10, 11, 12, 13, 14, 15, 16, 17, 18, 20, 21, 23, 24, 25, 26
Maurice, Jr. 142, 154
medical care in prison 242
meditation 163, 186, 200, 201
mental health challenges 67, 208
meritocracy 193
Mims, Gregory S. 180, 181
More Than Our Crimes 99, 242
Morrison, Toni 289
Moser, Ryan 52
motivations 48, 102, 110, 111, 208

Nixon, Richard 288, 290
Noah (aka Maaj) 198, 199, 202, 203, 209, 211, 215, 222; letters to 199–200, 202–5, 209–11, 215–19
Norton, Eleanor Holmes 21

Obama, Barack 131, 233, 284, 285, 286
Obamas, letter to 272–79
Orphaned Rebel Artistry, The 203

parenting different 153
parenting from prison, impact on children 51–55, 110–23
partnership, value of 41
penal system 46, 51, 88, 157, 208, 219, 270, 290

Petro, Lee 313, 314

philosophies and practice 195

Post Traumatic Slave Syndrome 47

Post Traumatic Slave Syndrome: America's Legacy of Enduring Injury and Healing (Leary) 262, 269

Prison Rape Elimination Act National Standards 271

prison reforms 25, 209, 233, 247, 284, 286, 287, 314, 320, 321

prison staff, opinions on 179–81

prison visitation 70, 313

Psychology Services Manual 295, 296

PTSD 318, 319

Public Enemy (band) 257

Quion 156, 157

reality 3, 25, 50, 62, 67, 101, 119, 150, 155, 156, 164, 167, 171, 182, 188, 189, 230, 235, 251, 256, 274, 275

recidivism 219, 230, 232, 233, 234, 270, 313, 317

rehabilitation, significance of 205, 226, 227, 264

religion 13, 55, 70, 74, 76, 77, 78, 125, 202

Residential Abuse Drug Program (RADP) 297

resignation, letter of 249–52

resilience 185, 186

Resource Centers 237

Richter, Robert, I. 1, 10, 11, 19; letter to 1–9

Salaam, Yusef 12, 13

Sargent, Edward D. 256

self-education 12, 17

self-study 60

sexual harassment 266, 271

sexual misconduct 261

Shirley 41, 44, 122

Soledad Brother (Jackson) 20

studies 15, 137, 154, 219, 224, 233, 237, 316

suicides 207

Suicide Watch Companion 297

Suicide Watch Inmate Companion Program 297

T 172, 173, 174, 176, 177, 181, 183, 185, 194, 202, 267; letters to, 142–44, 146–47, 149–50

Talib 79, 81, 83, 84, 159, 161, 162; letters to 159–61

Tawana 298, 299, 300, 301

Taylor, Shennel 307, 309, 311, 312, 314

Teresa 35, 36, 37; letters to 35–36

therapy group at Butner prison, finding of 24

13th (film) 46, 185

Thomson Correctional Center, Illinois 233

transformation, of Maurice 94

trauma 6, 21, 219, 261, 262, 263, 269, 270

Triny 170, 172; letters to 170–71

Trump, Donald 321

Unicor 266, 267, 268, 269

United States Penitentiary, Big Sandy 14, 70

United States Penitentiary, Hazelton 14, 99, 266, 291, 298

United States, Appellee v. Claude F. White, Jr., Airman Basic; U.S. Air Force, Appellant 295

Violent Crime Control and Law Enforcement Act 287

Wanda 37, 40, 67, 177; letter to 37–40

Washington, Booker T. 194

Welsing, Frances Cress 253, 254, 255, 256, 257

witness 45, 89, 148, 181, 184, 203

woman's perspective, understanding of 40

women, valuing 160

writers group, within the inmate community 60, 61

Yang, Crystal S. 243

young men's counseling group 40

zero-tolerance policy for drug-related crimes 290

www.ingramcontent.com/pod-product-compliance
Lightning Source LLC
Chambersburg PA
CBHW070749230426
43665CB00017B/2301